C000172477

I do

A PLANNER *for* YOUR PERFECT WEDDING DAY

Shelly Hagen

Adams Media
New York   London   Toronto   Sydney   New Delhi

This planner belongs to:

Adams Media
An Imprint of Simon & Schuster, LLC
100 Technology Center Drive
Stoughton, Massachusetts 02072

Copyright © 2024 by Simon & Schuster, LLC.

All rights reserved, including the right to reproduce this book or portions thereof in any form whatsoever. For information, address Adams Media Subsidiary Rights Department, 1230 Avenue of the Americas, New York, NY 10020.

First Adams Media hardcover edition December 2024

ADAMS MEDIA and colophon are registered trademarks of Simon & Schuster, LLC.

Simon & Schuster: Celebrating 100 Years of Publishing in 2024

For information about special discounts for bulk purchases, please contact Simon & Schuster Special Sales at 1-866-506-1949 or business@simonandschuster.com.

The Simon & Schuster Speakers Bureau can bring authors to your live event. For more information or to book an event, contact the Simon & Schuster Speakers Bureau at 1-866-248-3049 or visit our website at www.simonspeakers.com.

Interior design by Colleen Cunningham and Julia Jacintho
Hand lettering by Priscilla Yuen

Manufactured in China

10 9 8 7 6 5 4 3 2 1

ISBN 978-1-5072-2247-8

Many of the designations used by manufacturers and sellers to distinguish their products are claimed as trademarks. Where those designations appear in this book and Simon & Schuster, LLC, was aware of a trademark claim, the designations have been printed with initial capital letters.

Contains material adapted from the following title published by Adams Media, an Imprint of Simon & Schuster, LLC: *The Everything® Wedding Organizer, 5th Edition* by Shelly Hagen, copyright © 2016, ISBN 978-1-4405-9899-9.

Contents

Introduction

Congratulations! You're getting married! Now all you need to do is plan a wedding, an event that's most likely the biggest project you've ever had to organize. And naturally, you want your wedding to be an expression of your unique relationship. It can be overwhelming, but the best gift you can give yourself is in your hands—a wedding organizer to help you navigate the countless details between now and the big day.

Now that your excitement over the engagement is starting to settle down, it's time for you and your partner to take a breath and think about how you want your wedding to look. Do you want to go all out and create a spectacular day that will wow your friends and family, or are you thinking of a small, intimate affair with a curated guest list? Or something in between the two? How will you celebrate your personal love story?

No matter what the wedding of your dreams looks like, it's going to take a good amount of time, planning, and organization to get there. *I Do* will help you divide all the tasks into smaller, manageable parts. Each of the twenty chapters focuses on one of these tasks, from finding the perfect venue to designing invitations to planning your romantic last dance. Additionally, various checklists and worksheets cover all the wedding-planning basics, along with lots of extras. Use them all or just a few as you create a plan that reflects your perfect celebration.

The convenient, portable size of *I Do* means you can easily carry it in your bag to take notes wherever you are. Rate the dresses you try on, list the pros and cons of your top two venues, sketch out your ideal bouquet, or just jot down an idea when inspiration hits. This planner also includes sturdy pockets you can use to tuck in business cards, paper and fabric samples, magazine clippings, and photos. In time, this indispensable companion will become a lovely keepsake that will remind you and your love of the journey you took together—culminating in one extraordinary day.

CHAPTER 1

The Timeline

You're engaged—congratulations! You're on your way to Happily Ever After...right after you settle the little matter of the wedding. If you've started to look around for wedding ideas, you know there is an overwhelming amount of information out there, from wedding sites, social media, and bridal magazines to friends, coworkers, and family members. Even complete strangers will offer unsolicited advice when they learn you're newly engaged. Just remember that planning the big day is an individual thing, and when it comes to making the decisions, the opinions that matter most are yours and your partner's.

YOUR WEDDING STYLE

Before you get started with the work of wedding planning, take some time to discover and define your wedding style. Begin with your personal style. What kind of fashion are you drawn to? Which colors do you wear most often? How do you decorate your living space? Where do you like to vacation? Create an inspiration board (or three) on Pinterest or in a wedding app to collect images of tablescapes, decor, hairstyles, ceremony ideas, and attire that appeal to you. You can even borrow ideas from pre-created vision boards online. Soon, you'll see trends emerging that reveal your preferred style. You'll likely find that your preferences align with one or more of the following wedding styles:

TRADITIONAL/CLASSIC	Large bridal parties, neutral colors, a jazz trio
MODERN	Sleek decor, minimalist dresses, black accents
ROMANTIC	Lots of flowers, layered table settings, hand-lettered invitations
ELEGANT/GLAMOROUS	Black tie, luxurious venues, couture dresses
RUSTIC/DIY	Wildflowers, wooden elements, handmade decor
BOHO	Loosely arranged florals, patterned fabrics, lanterns
WHIMSICAL/THEMED	Nonmatching attire, pop culture themes, nontraditional rituals
COASTAL/BEACH	Waterfront ceremonies, seashell and coastal grass accents, relaxed attire
MINIMALIST	Small guest lists, intimate dinners, streamlined decor

SPREADING THE NEWS

There are several ways to share your exciting news with friends, family, and your community. The old-school way to spread the word is through a newspaper announcement. Typically, the newspaper announcement provides general information about the bride and groom, their schooling, careers, and so on. Many couples include an official engagement photo along with the announcement. Keep in mind that some newspapers charge a fee for this service. You may never have picked up a newspaper in your life, but your parents may still want to see you and your fiancé in print.

Save-the-date cards are great for notifying anyone outside of your immediate circle that they should mark their calendars. You can send these cards anywhere from a year to six months in advance, depending on when you're getting married (for example, May and June are big graduation and wedding months, and guests may book something else on your wedding weekend) or how excited you are to get the news out!

Setting up an engagement/wedding website is great for blogging about your engagement story, sharing wedding-planning updates, posting save-the-date announcements, uploading engagement photos, providing information about parties and registries, and generally giving a community feel to your upcoming wedding. There are plenty of low-cost and even free wedding site template companies online—a simple Internet search will provide you with an array of choices to use and begin creating and sharing instantly.

NEWSPAPER ENGAGEMENT ANNOUNCEMENT WORKSHEET

PUBLICATION NAME:

NAMES OF THE BRIDE'S PARENTS:

ADDRESS:

PHONE NUMBER:

Mr. and Mrs. _____ of _____ announce the
　　　　　　　(bride's parents' names)　　　　　　*(their city)*

engagement of their daughter, _____ , to _____ ,
　　　　　　　　　　　(bride's first and middle names)　　*(groom's first and last names)*

the son of Mr. and Mrs. _____ of _____ .
　　　　　　　　(groom's parents' names)　　　　　*(their city)*

A _____ wedding is planned. *(Or: No date has been set for the wedding.)*
　(month/season)

WEBSITE HOST WORKSHEET

WEBSITE NAME:

FEES: ☐ Yes ☐ No   FEE AMOUNT: $

TEMPLATE OPTIONS

SERVICES

☐ Guest list management

☐ Invitations

☐ Format and print address labels

☐ RSVP services

  ○ Basic (yes/no)

  ○ Complex (custom questions)

☐ Registry

  ○ On-site

  ○ Links

☐ Social media integration

☐ _____

☐ _____

NOTES

DO YOU NEED A WEDDING PLANNER?

Some couples choose to employ a wedding planner to help them coordinate the many details of the big event. Wedding planners (or consultants) have extensive knowledge, ideas, and contacts you might not have even thought of. Not everyone needs or wants a planner, and you shouldn't feel that you have to hire one just because someone else did. Some couples enjoy planning their own weddings and have plenty of time to do so. However, you may find that a consultant can relieve a great deal of the planning pressure you are facing, especially if you're short on time because of work obligations or tend to feel overwhelmed when planning a big project.

Once you find someone you might be interested in working with, schedule an appointment. Here are some questions to ask:

- How long have you been in business?
- Are you a full-time or part-time consultant?
- Do you have references?
- How many weddings do you plan in a typical month? On a typical weekend?
- What is the cost, how will you bill, and when will the final payment be due? (Hourly? Flat fee? Percentage?)
- What services are included in your quoted price?

The consultant you choose may offer different levels of service, ranging from helping you plan the entire event down to the tiniest detail or simply scoping out reception locations and caterers. Don't forget to check references. Ask previous clients to elaborate on their experience: what was fabulous, what didn't go according to plan, and how the consultant handled problems or last-minute surprises.

PRE-WEDDING CHECKLIST

Here's the big list—all of the things you may need to do between now and the big day. Of course, depending on the type of wedding you're planning, you may ignore some items or add others, but this will give you a general idea of what you should do each step of the way.

SIX TO TWELVE MONTHS BEFORE THE WEDDING

- ○ Decide on type and style of wedding.
- ○ Decide on time of day.
- ○ Choose the location.
- ○ Set a date.
- ○ Set a budget.
- ○ Select bridal party.
- ○ Plan color scheme.
- ○ Select and order bridal gown.
- ○ Select and order headpiece.
- ○ Select and order shoes.
- ○ Select and order attendants' attire.
- ○ Book officiant (for a civil ceremony).
- ○ Start honeymoon planning.

- ○ Start gift registry.
- ○ Start compiling guest list.
- ○ Select caterer.
- ○ Select band or DJ.
- ○ Select florist.
- ○ Select photographer/ videographer.
- ○ Start planning reception.
- ○ Reserve venue for reception.
- ○ Select and order wedding rings.
- ○ Reserve accommodations for guests.
- ○ Select and order attire for groomsmen and groom.
- ○ Send save-the-date cards.

THREE TO FOUR MONTHS BEFORE THE WEDDING

- ○ Complete guest list.
- ○ Plan to have mothers choose attire.
- ○ Select and order invitations.
- ○ Order personal stationery.
- ○ Finalize reception arrangements. (Rent items such as tents, tables, or chairs now.)
- ○ Make reservations for honeymoon.
- ○ Confirm dress delivery.
- ○ Confirm time and date with florist.
- ○ Order cake.
- ○ Confirm time and date with caterer.
- ○ Confirm time and date with photographer/videographer.
- ○ Confirm time and date with band or DJ.
- ○ Confirm time and date with wedding site.
- ○ Discuss transportation to and from ceremony and reception.
- ○ Schedule fittings for groom and groomsmen.
- ○ Schedule bridesmaids' dress fittings.

SIX TO EIGHT WEEKS BEFORE THE WEDDING

- ○ Mail invitations.
- ○ Make appointment to get marriage license.
- ○ Finalize honeymoon arrangements.
- ○ Schedule hair and makeup application.
- ○ Schedule bridesmaids' luncheon or party.
- ○ Plan rehearsal and rehearsal dinner.
- ○ Schedule bridal photo shoot.

ONE MONTH BEFORE THE WEDDING

○ Begin to record gifts received and send thank-you notes.

○ Send bridal portrait with announcement to newspaper.

○ Purchase gifts for bridal party.

○ Purchase gift for fiancé if you are exchanging gifts.

○ Book trial appointments with hair and makeup stylists.

○ Schedule final dress fitting, including accessories and shoes.

○ Get marriage license.

TWO WEEKS BEFORE THE WEDDING

○ Finalize wedding day transportation.

○ Arrange to change name on driver's license, Social Security card, etc.

○ Confirm any accommodations for the guests.

○ Prepare wedding announcements to be mailed after the wedding.

○ Plan reception seating arrangements.

ONE WEEK BEFORE THE WEDDING

○ Finalize the number of guests with the caterer and venue.

○ Confirm desired shots with photographer.

○ Arrange for one last fitting for wedding attire.

○ Make sure rings are picked up and fit properly.

○ Confirm receipt of marriage license.

○ Have rehearsal and rehearsal dinner (one or two days before wedding).

○ Reconfirm plans with officiant, reception site coordinator, photographer, videographer, band or DJ, florist, baker, limousine company, and hairstylist/makeup artist.

○ Reconfirm honeymoon travel arrangements and hotel reservations.

○ Reconfirm hotel reservation for your wedding night.

○ Start packing for the honeymoon.

○ Give your wedding rings and marriage license to your honor attendants to hold until the ceremony.

○ Make sure groom and best man have enough cash for tipping.

○ Give an "emergency repair kit" (safety pins, extra hosiery, tissues, aspirin, etc.) to a trusted attendant.

ON YOUR WEDDING DAY

○ Try to relax and pamper yourself.

○ Eat at least one small meal.

○ Have your hair and makeup done several hours before the ceremony.

○ Start dressing one to two hours before the ceremony.

CHAPTER 2

The Budget

After you decide on the type of wedding you want, you'll need to figure out exactly how you're going to pay for it. The amount you allocate will help you determine the number of guests you can invite, the location of your reception, the food you choose, the number of photographs you will have taken, the type and number of flowers and centerpieces, and, really, just about every other element of the celebration.

2

There are two ways of setting a budget. The first is to determine the amount of money that's available to you right now. This will include any money that you and your fiancé may have saved for the event, as well as any contributions from your parents or other family members that you're expecting. The total amount of these resources is your budget—assuming you're planning to pay cash for the bulk of your wedding expenses.

Another way to go about this—especially if you're pretty sure your parents will want to chip in to defray your costs, but you're unsure of how generous they plan on being—is to try tallying up the cost of your ideal wedding before asking for financial assistance. You may find that you'll get a better response if you have an estimate, rather than just asking for a contribution. The Wedding Budget Worksheet will be a valuable resource to you in this regard because it will give you a good idea of how much services and items in an average wedding cost.

You'll need to do your homework. If you have friends who have been married recently, don't be shy about asking them how much they paid for things. Most newlyweds are happy to pass on the wisdom they gained from going through the wedding-planning experience themselves.

Once you've consulted your friends, pick up the phone. Call (or email) several reception sites and caterers and ask for their wedding menus to get an estimate of the per-person rates or their minimum charge for an event. Be sure to ask about any additional fees they may charge (such as rental fees, set-up fees, gratuity, corkage, or cake-cutting fees). Do the same with photographers, limousine services, videographers, and so on.

Once you have the estimates, you can insert cost ranges into the Wedding Budget Worksheet to give you a "cheapest to costliest" scenario. Then you can find the average price of each item and figure out which services are most important to you. Maybe it's more important for you to have a top-of-the-line photographer and just a fairly average cake (or vice versa!). Using this worksheet will help you figure out where your wedding dollars are best spent.

WEDDING BUDGET WORKSHEET

ITEM	PROJECTED COST	DEPOSIT PAID	BALANCE DUE	WHO PAYS?
WEDDING CONSULTANT				
FEE	$	$	$	
TIP (usually 15–20%)	$	$	$	
PRE-WEDDING PARTIES				
ENGAGEMENT PARTY (if hosted by bride and groom)				
SITE RENTAL	$	$	$	
EQUIPMENT RENTAL	$	$	$	
INVITATIONS	$	$	$	
FOOD	$	$	$	
BEVERAGES	$	$	$	
DECORATIONS	$	$	$	
FLOWERS	$	$	$	
PARTY FAVORS	$	$	$	
BRIDESMAIDS' PARTY/LUNCHEON				
FOOD	$	$	$	
BEVERAGES	$	$	$	
DECORATIONS	$	$	$	
FLOWERS	$	$	$	
PARTY FAVORS	$	$	$	
REHEARSAL DINNER (if hosted by bride and groom)				
SITE RENTAL	$	$	$	
EQUIPMENT RENTAL	$	$	$	
INVITATIONS	$	$	$	
FOOD	$	$	$	
BEVERAGES	$	$	$	
DECORATIONS	$	$	$	
FLOWERS	$	$	$	
PARTY FAVORS	$	$	$	

ITEM	PROJECTED COST	DEPOSIT PAID	BALANCE DUE	WHO PAYS?
CEREMONY				
LOCATION FEE	$	$	$	
OFFICIANT'S FEE	$	$	$	
DONATION (optional)	$	$	$	
ORGANIST/ON-SITE MUSICIAN	$	$	$	
TIP (amount varies)	$	$	$	
OTHER MUSICIANS	$	$	$	
TIP (amount varies)	$	$	$	
PROGRAM	$	$	$	
BUSINESS AND LEGAL MATTERS				
MARRIAGE LICENSE	$	$	$	
BLOOD TEST (if applicable)	$	$	$	
WEDDING JEWELRY				
BRIDE'S WEDDING BAND	$	$	$	
GROOM'S WEDDING BAND	$	$	$	
BRIDE'S ATTIRE				
WEDDING GOWN	$	$	$	
ALTERATIONS	$	$	$	
UNDERGARMENTS	$	$	$	
VEIL	$	$	$	
SHOES	$	$	$	
JEWELRY (excluding wedding ring)	$	$	$	
MAKEUP ARTIST	$	$	$	
HAIRSTYLIST	$	$	$	
NAIL TECHNICIAN	$	$	$	

ITEM	PROJECTED COST	DEPOSIT PAID	BALANCE DUE	WHO PAYS?
GROOM'S FORMALWEAR				
TUXEDO	$	$	$	
SHOES	$	$	$	
GIFTS				
BRIDE'S ATTENDANTS	$	$	$	
GROOM'S ATTENDANTS	$	$	$	
BRIDE (optional)	$	$	$	
GROOM (optional)	$	$	$	
RECEPTION				
SITE RENTAL	$	$	$	
EQUIPMENT RENTAL (chairs, tent, etc.)	$	$	$	
DECORATIONS	$	$	$	
SERVERS, BARTENDERS	$	$	$	
WINE SERVICE FOR COCKTAIL HOUR	$	$	$	
HORS D'OEUVRES	$	$	$	
ENTRÉES	$	$	$	
MEALS FOR VENDORS	$	$	$	
NONALCOHOLIC BEVERAGES	$	$	$	
WINE	$	$	$	
CHAMPAGNE	$	$	$	
LIQUOR	$	$	$	
DESSERT	$	$	$	
GUEST BOOK	$	$	$	
PLACE CARDS	$	$	$	
PRINTED NAPKINS	$	$	$	

ITEM	PROJECTED COST	DEPOSIT PAID	BALANCE DUE	WHO PAYS?
GUEST FAVORS	$	$	$	
TIP FOR CATERER OR BANQUET MANAGER (usually 15–20%)	$	$	$	
TIP FOR SERVERS, BARTENDERS (usually 15–20% total)	$	$	$	
RECEPTION MUSIC				
MUSICIANS FOR COCKTAIL HOUR	$	$	$	
TIP (optional, up to 15%)	$	$	$	
LIVE BAND	$	$	$	
TIP (optional, usually $25 per band member)	$	$	$	
DISC JOCKEY	$	$	$	
TIP (optional, usually 15–20%)	$	$	$	
PHOTOGRAPHY AND VIDEOGRAPHY				
ENGAGEMENT PHOTO SHOOT	$	$	$	
WEDDING PORTRAIT	$	$	$	
WEDDING PROOFS	$	$	$	
PHOTOGRAPHER'S FEE	$	$	$	
ALBUM	$	$	$	
MOTHERS' ALBUMS	$	$	$	
EXTRA PRINTS	$	$	$	
VIDEOGRAPHER'S FEE	$	$	$	

2

WEDDING BUDGET WORKSHEET (CONTINUED)

ITEM	PROJECTED COST	DEPOSIT PAID	BALANCE DUE	WHO PAYS?
FLOWERS AND DECORATIONS				
FLOWERS FOR WEDDING SITE	$	$	$	
DECORATIONS FOR WEDDING SITE	$	$	$	
BRIDE'S BOUQUET	$	$	$	
BRIDESMAIDS' FLOWERS	$	$	$	
BOUTONNIERES	$	$	$	
CORSAGES	$	$	$	
FLOWERS FOR RECEPTION SITE	$	$	$	
POTTED PLANTS	$	$	$	
TABLE CENTERPIECES	$	$	$	
HEAD TABLE	$	$	$	
CAKE TABLE	$	$	$	
DECORATIONS FOR RECEPTION	$	$	$	
WEDDING INVITATIONS AND STATIONERY				
INVITATIONS	$	$	$	
ANNOUNCEMENTS	$	$	$	
SAVE THE DATE	$	$	$	
THANK-YOU NOTES	$	$	$	
CALLIGRAPHER	$	$	$	
POSTAGE (for invitations and response cards)	$	$	$	

2

WEDDING BUDGET WORKSHEET (CONTINUED)

ITEM	PROJECTED COST	DEPOSIT PAID	BALANCE DUE	WHO PAYS?
WEDDING CAKES				
WEDDING CAKE	$	$	$	
GROOM'S CAKE	$	$	$	
FLOWERS FOR CAKE	$	$	$	
WEDDING TRANSPORTATION				
LIMOUSINES OR RENTED CARS	$	$	$	
PARKING	$	$	$	
TIP FOR DRIVERS (usually 15–20%)	$	$	$	
GUEST TRANSPORTATION	$	$	$	
HONEYMOON				
TRANSPORTATION	$	$	$	
ACCOMMODATIONS	$	$	$	
MEALS	$	$	$	
SPENDING MONEY	$	$	$	
ADDITIONAL EXPENSES				
	$	$	$	
	$	$	$	
	$	$	$	
	$	$	$	
	$	$	$	
	$	$	$	
	$	$	$	
	$	$	$	
	$	$	$	
	$	$	$	

WEDDING BUDGET WORKSHEET (CONTINUED)

ITEM	PROJECTED COST	DEPOSIT PAID	BALANCE DUE	WHO PAYS?
ADDITIONAL EXPENSES CONT.				
	$	$	$	
	$	$	$	
	$	$	$	
	$	$	$	
	$	$	$	
	$	$	$	
	$	$	$	
Total of All Expenses:			$	

CHAPTER 3

The Wedding Party

Your wedding party can be as big—or as small—as you like. Formal weddings usually have a larger number of attendants than informal ones, but you can feel free to bend tradition here if you think it's appropriate. Brides often feel obligated to have certain people in the wedding, even if they're not that close to them. However, if you surround yourself with family members and close friends whom you can depend on, you may discover that those pre-wedding parties, fittings, and rehearsals will go more smoothly than you expected.

CHOOSING BRIDESMAIDS AND GROOMSMEN

Think about which of your close friends and family members you and your fiancé would really like to have in the wedding. Traditionally, there are an equal number of bridesmaids and groomsmen, but there is no reason to adhere to this rule. The general guideline is one groomsman for every fifty guests so that guests can be ushered to their ceremony seats in an orderly fashion.

As soon as you figure out whom you want to include in your wedding party, ask them! Sometimes, due to monetary problems or other conflicts, one of your first choices may have to decline, and you want to make sure you have enough time to ask a replacement. Some brides like to make this an elaborate event, complete with bridesmaid "proposal" gift boxes. If that's up your alley, go for it. If you want to save some money, it's perfectly acceptable to simply ask if they would like to be in your wedding.

ATTENDANTS' DUTIES

Here's a rundown of which attendants do what in a traditional wedding.

MAID OR MATRON OF HONOR

- Helps with addressing invitation envelopes
- Helps with recording wedding gifts
- Plans the bachelorette party
- Plans a shower with the bridesmaids
- Helps the bride dress for the ceremony
- Holds the bride's bouquet during the vows
- Signs the wedding certificate with the best man
- Helps the bride change clothes after the reception and takes care of the bridal gown

BEST MAN

- Organizes the bachelor party
- Gets the groom to the ceremony
- Pays the officiant just before or after the ceremony
- Holds the bride's wedding ring until it's needed during the ceremony

BRIDESMAIDS

- Help plan the bachelorette party and shower
- Keep a record of shower gifts during the party
- Assist the maid of honor with pre-wedding shopping or tasks
- Help the bride get ready for the ceremony

GROOMSMEN

- Arrive early to assist with the setup and finishing touches
- Escort guests to their seats
- Meet, welcome, and seat guests of honor (such as grandparents)
- Roll out the aisle runner
- Oversee the transfer of the gifts to a secure location after the reception

BRIDE'S ATTENDANTS CONTACT WORKSHEET

MAID/MATRON OF HONOR

NAME:

ADDRESS:

PHONE: EMAIL:

SPECIAL DUTIES:

BRIDESMAIDS

NAME:

ADDRESS:

PHONE: EMAIL:

SPECIAL DUTIES

NAME:

ADDRESS:

PHONE: EMAIL:

SPECIAL DUTIES

NAME:

ADDRESS:

PHONE: EMAIL:

SPECIAL DUTIES

BRIDE'S ATTENDANTS CONTACT WORKSHEET (CONTINUED)

FLOWER GIRL

NAME:

ADDRESS:

PHONE: EMAIL:

SPECIAL DUTIES

OTHER HONOR ATTENDANTS

NAME:

ADDRESS:

PHONE: EMAIL:

SPECIAL DUTIES

NAME:

ADDRESS:

PHONE: EMAIL:

SPECIAL DUTIES

NAME:

ADDRESS:

PHONE: EMAIL:

SPECIAL DUTIES

GROOM'S ATTENDANTS CONTACT WORKSHEET

3

BEST MAN

NAME:

ADDRESS:

PHONE: EMAIL:

SPECIAL DUTIES

USHERS

NAME:

ADDRESS:

PHONE: EMAIL:

SPECIAL DUTIES

NAME:

ADDRESS:

PHONE: EMAIL:

SPECIAL DUTIES

NAME:

ADDRESS:

PHONE: EMAIL:

SPECIAL DUTIES

RING BEARER

NAME:

ADDRESS:

PHONE: EMAIL:

SPECIAL DUTIES

3

OTHER HONOR ATTENDANTS

NAME:

ADDRESS:

PHONE: EMAIL:

SPECIAL DUTIES

NAME:

ADDRESS:

PHONE: EMAIL:

SPECIAL DUTIES

NAME:

ADDRESS:

PHONE: EMAIL:

SPECIAL DUTIES

GIFTS FOR THE WEDDING PARTY

It's customary to show your gratitude to the wedding party by giving each member a little gift. Let everyone know you appreciate all the time and money they've spent helping make your wedding day something you'll all enjoy and remember.

GIFT IDEAS FOR THE BRIDESMAIDS

○ Jewelry

○ A personalized robe

○ Perfume or luxury bath products

○ A monogrammed jewelry or cosmetic case

GIFT IDEAS FOR THE GROOMSMEN

○ A money clip or wallet

○ Initialed cuff links

○ Matching sunglasses

○ A monogrammed travel or shaving kit

GIFT IDEAS ANY ATTENDANT WOULD LOVE

○ Gift certificate for a restaurant, spa, or local shop

○ An engraved flask

○ A bottle of good wine or top-shelf liquor

○ Wine or beer glasses

WEDDING PARTY GIFT IDEAS

MAID/MATRON OF HONOR

BEST MAN

BRIDESMAIDS

USHERS

OTHER

3

CHAPTER 4

The Guest List

Setting out to create your guest list sounds easy enough, at least until you sit down and try to do it. Then you realize that your mother wants to invite relatives you've never met, and all of your coworkers think they're coming. The smartest strategy for addressing these problems is to hit them head-on. Don't try to ignore them or push them aside until the last minute.

MAKING THE LIST

Start out by listing everyone you'd ideally like to invite. It may turn out that the total number is not that far beyond your reach. If you do end up having to shorten the list, set boundaries and stick to them. In most cases, the guest list is divided evenly between the two families, regardless of who is paying for what. Couples often split the list three ways: the bride's parents' guests, the groom's parents' guests, and the couple's friends.

Don't forget to include your attendants and your officiant (and his or her spouse).

	NAME	ADDRESS	TELEPHONE	RSVP RECD.?
1.				☐
2.				☐
3.				☐
4.				☐
5.				☐
6.				☐
7.				☐
8.				☐
9.				☐
10.				☐
11.				☐
12.				☐
13.				☐
14.				☐

GUEST LIST WORKSHEET

	NAME	ADDRESS	TELEPHONE	RSVP RECD.?
15.				☐
16.				☐
17.				☐
18.				☐
19.				☐
20.				☐
21.				☐
22.				☐
23.				☐
24.				☐
25.				☐
26.				☐
27.				☐
28.				☐
29.				☐
30.				☐
31.				☐
32.				☐
33.				☐
34.				☐
35.				☐
36.				☐
37.				☐

4

	NAME	ADDRESS	TELEPHONE	RSVP RECD.?
38.				☐
39.				☐
40.				☐
41.				☐
42.				☐
43.				☐
44.				☐
45.				☐
46.				☐
47.				☐
48.				☐
49.				☐
50.				☐
51.				☐
52.				☐
53.				☐
54.				☐
55.				☐
56.				☐
57.				☐
58.				☐
59.				☐
60.				☐

NAME	ADDRESS	TELEPHONE	RSVP RECD.?
61.			☐
62.			☐
63.			☐
64.			☐
65.			☐
66.			☐
67.			☐
68.			☐
69.			☐
70.			☐
71.			☐
72.			☐
73.			☐
74.			☐
75.			☐
76.			☐
77.			☐
78.			☐
79.			☐
80.			☐
81.			☐
82.			☐
83.			☐

4

	NAME	ADDRESS	TELEPHONE	RSVP RECD.?
84.				☐
85.				☐
86.				☐
87.				☐
88.				☐
89.				☐
90.				☐
91.				☐
92.				☐
93.				☐
94.				☐
95.				☐
96.				☐
97.				☐
98.				☐
99.				☐
100.				☐
101.				☐
102.				☐
103.				☐
104.				☐
105.				☐
106.				☐

	NAME	ADDRESS	TELEPHONE	RSVP RECD.?
107.				☐
108.				☐
109.				☐
110.				☐
111.				☐
112.				☐
113.				☐
114.				☐
115.				☐
116.				☐
117.				☐
118.				☐
119.				☐
120.				☐
121.				☐
122.				☐
123.				☐
124.				☐
125.				☐
126.				☐
127.				☐
128.				☐
129.				☐

	NAME	ADDRESS	TELEPHONE	RSVP RECD.?
130.				☐
131.				☐
132.				☐
133.				☐
134.				☐
135.				☐
136.				☐
137.				☐
138.				☐
139.				☐
140.				☐
141.				☐
142.				☐
143.				☐
144.				☐
145.				☐
146.				☐
147.				☐
148.				☐
149.				☐
150.				☐

4

Some guests will be traveling to be with you on the big day, so you should try to make things as pleasant and convenient for them as possible. Start by helping them find a place to stay. Guests pay for their own lodging (unless either the bride's or groom's family offers to pick up the tab), but it is customary for you to provide information so that guests can make their own reservations. Try to find a reasonably priced hotel or two that is close to your venue. Most hotels will offer a lower rate for a block of rooms. Grouping your out-of-town guests in one hotel has several advantages:

○ The group rates will be less expensive.

○ They can carpool to and from the festivities.

○ They can mingle with the other guests during the downtime.

Though grouping everyone at the same hotel is preferable, some guests may not be able to afford the hotel you choose. Others may have specific preferences—or may simply want their privacy. It's a good idea to compile a short list of other options for guests who may need them.

GUEST ACCOMMODATIONS WORKSHEET

BLOCKS OF ROOMS RESERVED FOR WEDDING AT

HOTEL NAME:

ADDRESS:

WEBSITE:

PHONE: EMAIL:

CONTACT:

RESERVATION NUMBER:

APPROXIMATE DISTANCE FROM

CEREMONY SITE: RECEPTION SITE:

ROOM INFORMATION

NUMBER OF SINGLE ROOMS RESERVED:

SINGLE ROOM DAILY RATE: $

NUMBER OF DOUBLE ROOMS RESERVED:

DOUBLE ROOM DAILY RATE: $

TOTAL NUMBER OF ROOMS RESERVED IN BLOCK:

IMPORTANT DATES

DATE(S) RESERVED:

CUTOFF/LAST DAY RESERVATIONS ACCEPTED:

TERMS OF AGREEMENT

PAYMENT PROCEDURE

NOTES

ALTERNATIVE NEARBY LODGING (OPTION 1)

HOTEL NAME:

ADDRESS:

WEBSITE:

PHONE: EMAIL:

CONTACT:

RESERVATION NUMBER:

APPROXIMATE DISTANCE FROM

CEREMONY SITE: RECEPTION SITE:

NOTES

ALTERNATIVE NEARBY LODGING (OPTION 2)

HOTEL NAME:

ADDRESS:

WEBSITE:

PHONE: EMAIL:

CONTACT:

RESERVATION NUMBER:

APPROXIMATE DISTANCE FROM

CEREMONY SITE: RECEPTION SITE:

NOTES

HOSPITALITY GIFTS

With folks traveling to attend your wedding, it's great to include a gift bag or basket full of treats or small gifts to say thank you and help guests enjoy their stay. These welcome totes can be tailored to your specific event and add an extra personal touch. Whether you are looking to get creative on a budget or splurge on your guests, you can make a memorable tote or basket for your special day. Here are some ideas to get you started:

- ○ A canvas tote or decorative basket is a beautiful item your guests can reuse after the day, and they'll be reminded of your wedding each time they use it.

- ○ Tuck in a note that expresses your appreciation for sharing the day with you.

- ○ Include a schedule of events for your guests to follow, along with information about transportation.

- ○ If the wedding will take place outdoors, include practical items such as sunscreen, bottled water, or bug spray. Fun sunglasses or folding fans are great too!

- ○ Provide local treats or keepsakes.

- ○ Drinks (alcoholic or nonalcoholic) are a great way to set the tone for the celebrations to come and can help guests cut down on hotel expenses.

- ○ Provide fresh fruit and fun snacks for pre- and post-wedding gatherings. Include a range of salty and sweet treats for guests to munch on.

HOSPITALITY GIFT IDEAS

CONTAINERS:	NUMBER NEEDED OF EACH:
☐ Baskets	
☐ Boxes	
☐ Gift bags	
☐ Other:	
☐ Other:	

CONTENTS

HOTEL CONTACT INFORMATION

CONTACT: PHONE:

SPECIAL INSTRUCTIONS

NOTES

CHAPTER 5

The Registry

Need them or not, you will receive many gifts when you get married. Whether your house is already fully stocked or you need everything, registering for gifts is an easy way to let people know what you really want and will use. With online registries especially, shopping (and shipping) could not possibly be any easier. And that's why you'll be writing thank-you notes until your hand cramps.

STORE REGISTRIES

Creating a gift registry is a free service provided by many big-box, jewelry, gift, and specialty stores. You and your fiancé get to spend an afternoon in the store choosing the things you want (yes, it's as fun as it sounds). When friends and family go into these stores, pulling up your registry is as easy as finding the touchscreen computer that contains the information. Registries are usually also available online as part of a store's website. Each purchase is noted on the registry to avoid duplicate gifts.

Although you can register for a few choice items at a small local boutique, it's best to register with at least one national store as well. Your registry will be available at the store branches in other cities and states and will appear on the store's website—all key advantages, especially for out-of-town guests.

STORE GIFT REGISTRIES WORKSHEET

STORE #1

STORE NAME: WEBSITE:

NAME(S) REGISTRY LISTED UNDER:

LOCATIONS

NOTES

5

STORE #2

STORE NAME: WEBSITE:

NAME(S) REGISTRY LISTED UNDER:

LOCATIONS

NOTES

STORE #3

STORE NAME: WEBSITE:

NAME(S) REGISTRY LISTED UNDER:

LOCATIONS

NOTES

ONLINE GIFT REGISTRIES

Websites like Zola, MyRegistry, Amazon, Thankful, Traveler's Joy, and Honeyfund allow guests to choose from a myriad of gifts to give, from the traditional kitchen, bath, and dining options to curated experiences and more unique contributions toward your honeymoon. Guests can buy you dinner and drinks at the resort you plan to visit; treat you to a fun experience like snorkeling, a wine tasting, or spa treatments; or contribute to online funds that can go toward a trip abroad, your future home, or other larger-ticket items. Your wedding website host may also include online registry options.

Online registries track shipping and exchanges for you, and some will even let you decide when you'd like your gift delivered. Because so many options can be found in just one place with these sites, you will find all of the brands and products you prefer, and your guests will enjoy choosing from an assortment of gifts and have more opportunities to give something personal.

Be sure to include links to all gift registries on your wedding website.

ONLINE GIFT REGISTRIES WORKSHEET

ONLINE STORE #1

STORE NAME: _____ WEBSITE: _____

NAME(S) REGISTRY IS LISTED UNDER: _____

Linked to wedding website?　☐ Yes　☐ No

NOTES

ONLINE STORE #2

STORE NAME: _____ WEBSITE: _____

NAME(S) REGISTRY IS LISTED UNDER: _____

Linked to wedding website?　☐ Yes　☐ No

NOTES

ONLINE STORE #3

STORE NAME: _____ WEBSITE: _____

NAME(S) REGISTRY IS LISTED UNDER: _____

Linked to wedding website?　☐ Yes　☐ No

NOTES

THANK-YOU NOTES

As soon as you receive a gift, you should send out a thank-you note. As hard as it will be considering the many notes you'll be writing, try to be warm and personal in all of them. Always mention the gift and, if possible, how you and your fiancé will be using it. This small touch will prevent people from feeling that you just sent them a form letter (which, by the way, is completely unacceptable, no matter how busy you are). Don't forget to keep track of your gifts and thank-you notes so you don't end up questioning whether you already thanked your great-aunt for her generous donation to your honeymoon fund!

The Shower

(and Other Pre-Wedding Parties)

6

One perk of following the traditional road to your wedding day is that you'll suddenly find yourself in the middle of a gift-giving storm. Although you won't be throwing a party for yourself, whoever hosts your shower or engagement party will probably be looking for your opinion on any number of issues, such as the guest list, the menu, and games.

THE ENGAGEMENT PARTY

Although it is customary for the family of the bride to host some sort of an engagement party, it's perfectly acceptable for the family of the groom or a friend to host such an affair—or for you to do without one altogether if you prefer. Most engagement parties are informal, with invites being done via phone calls or evites. The party is usually held either at the host's home or in a restaurant. Some guests may bring a gift.

6

ENGAGEMENT PARTY GUEST LIST WORKSHEET

NAME:

ADDRESS:

PHONE:

EMAIL:

☐ RSVP   NUMBER IN PARTY:

NAME:

ADDRESS:

PHONE:

EMAIL:

☐ RSVP   NUMBER IN PARTY:

NAME:

ADDRESS:

PHONE:

EMAIL:

☐ RSVP   NUMBER IN PARTY:

NAME:

ADDRESS:

PHONE:

EMAIL:

☐ RSVP   NUMBER IN PARTY:

NAME:

ADDRESS:

PHONE:

EMAIL:

☐ RSVP   NUMBER IN PARTY:

NAME:

ADDRESS:

PHONE:

EMAIL:

☐ RSVP   NUMBER IN PARTY:

NAME:

ADDRESS:

PHONE:

EMAIL:

☐ RSVP   NUMBER IN PARTY:

NAME:

ADDRESS:

PHONE:

EMAIL:

☐ RSVP   NUMBER IN PARTY:

NAME:

ADDRESS:

PHONE:

EMAIL:

☐ RSVP   NUMBER IN PARTY:

NAME:

ADDRESS:

PHONE:

EMAIL:

☐ RSVP   NUMBER IN PARTY:

6

6

NAME:	NAME:
ADDRESS:	ADDRESS:
PHONE:	PHONE:
EMAIL:	EMAIL:
☐ RSVP NUMBER IN PARTY:	☐ RSVP NUMBER IN PARTY:
NAME:	NAME:
ADDRESS:	ADDRESS:
PHONE:	PHONE:
EMAIL:	EMAIL:
☐ RSVP NUMBER IN PARTY:	☐ RSVP NUMBER IN PARTY:
NAME:	NAME:
ADDRESS:	ADDRESS:
PHONE:	PHONE:
EMAIL:	EMAIL:
☐ RSVP NUMBER IN PARTY:	☐ RSVP NUMBER IN PARTY:
NAME:	NAME:
ADDRESS:	ADDRESS:
PHONE:	PHONE:
EMAIL:	EMAIL:
☐ RSVP NUMBER IN PARTY:	☐ RSVP NUMBER IN PARTY:
NAME:	NAME:
ADDRESS:	ADDRESS:
PHONE:	PHONE:
EMAIL:	EMAIL:
☐ RSVP NUMBER IN PARTY:	☐ RSVP NUMBER IN PARTY:

NAME:

ADDRESS:

PHONE:

EMAIL:

☐ RSVP   NUMBER IN PARTY:

NAME:

ADDRESS:

PHONE:

EMAIL:

☐ RSVP   NUMBER IN PARTY:

NAME:

ADDRESS:

PHONE:

EMAIL:

☐ RSVP   NUMBER IN PARTY:

NAME:

ADDRESS:

PHONE:

EMAIL:

☐ RSVP   NUMBER IN PARTY:

NAME:

ADDRESS:

PHONE:

EMAIL:

☐ RSVP   NUMBER IN PARTY:

NAME:

ADDRESS:

PHONE:

EMAIL:

☐ RSVP   NUMBER IN PARTY:

NAME:

ADDRESS:

PHONE:

EMAIL:

☐ RSVP   NUMBER IN PARTY:

NAME:

ADDRESS:

PHONE:

EMAIL:

☐ RSVP   NUMBER IN PARTY:

NAME:

ADDRESS:

PHONE:

EMAIL:

☐ RSVP   NUMBER IN PARTY:

NAME:

ADDRESS:

PHONE:

EMAIL:

☐ RSVP   NUMBER IN PARTY:

6

ENGAGEMENT PARTY GIFT RECORDER

NAME	DESCRIPTION OF GIFT	THANK-YOU NOTE SENT?
		☐
		☐
		☐
		☐
		☐
		☐
		☐
		☐
		☐
		☐
		☐
		☐
		☐
		☐
		☐
		☐

6

ENGAGEMENT PARTY GIFT RECORDER (CONTINUED)

NAME	DESCRIPTION OF GIFT	THANK-YOU NOTE SENT?
		☐
		☐
		☐
		☐
		☐
		☐
		☐
		☐
		☐
		☐
		☐
		☐
		☐
		☐
		☐
		☐

6

THE BRIDAL SHOWER

This is the big pre-wedding party. Family, friends, coworkers, or anyone else who is so inclined can throw a shower for you. Usually your attendants, in combination with your mother and other family members, will work together to host a shower—but who knows what other generous people might have a party up their sleeve?

Typically, a shower is held at a restaurant, a small function hall, or in someone's home, depending on the size of the guest list. In the past, this was an event strictly for women, but it's common now for the fiancé to join the festivities. "Jack and Jill" showers—where attendants from both sides host and attend—are also becoming more common.

Showers are usually held two to three months before the wedding date. If you absolutely cannot corral your most important guests within the confines of this period, shoot for a slightly earlier date (say, three and a half months before the ceremony)—or one that's a little closer to the wedding. But a date that's *too* close to the wedding might set you up for feeling stressed over last-minute details while trying to squeeze your shower in.

THE GUEST LIST

If you plan for your shower to be a small, informal affair in someone's tiny apartment, your list will obviously be much different than if the shower is going to be in a huge banquet hall. In either case, who should be invited, and who should be left off the list? The cardinal rule is that any guest who is invited to the shower is automatically invited to the wedding. Make sure that your hosts are only inviting preapproved wedding guests.

BRIDAL SHOWER GUEST LIST WORKSHEET

NAME:

ADDRESS:

PHONE:

EMAIL:

☐ RSVP   NUMBER IN PARTY:

NAME:

ADDRESS:

PHONE:

EMAIL:

☐ RSVP   NUMBER IN PARTY:

NAME:

ADDRESS:

PHONE:

EMAIL:

☐ RSVP   NUMBER IN PARTY:

NAME:

ADDRESS:

PHONE:

EMAIL:

☐ RSVP   NUMBER IN PARTY:

NAME:

ADDRESS:

PHONE:

EMAIL:

☐ RSVP   NUMBER IN PARTY:

NAME:

ADDRESS:

PHONE:

EMAIL:

☐ RSVP   NUMBER IN PARTY:

NAME:

ADDRESS:

PHONE:

EMAIL:

☐ RSVP   NUMBER IN PARTY:

NAME:

ADDRESS:

PHONE:

EMAIL:

☐ RSVP   NUMBER IN PARTY:

NAME:

ADDRESS:

PHONE:

EMAIL:

☐ RSVP   NUMBER IN PARTY:

NAME:

ADDRESS:

PHONE:

EMAIL:

☐ RSVP   NUMBER IN PARTY:

6

NAME:	NAME:
ADDRESS:	ADDRESS:
PHONE:	PHONE:
EMAIL:	EMAIL:
☐ RSVP NUMBER IN PARTY:	☐ RSVP NUMBER IN PARTY:
NAME:	NAME:
ADDRESS:	ADDRESS:
PHONE:	PHONE:
EMAIL:	EMAIL:
☐ RSVP NUMBER IN PARTY:	☐ RSVP NUMBER IN PARTY:
NAME:	NAME:
ADDRESS:	ADDRESS:
PHONE:	PHONE:
EMAIL:	EMAIL:
☐ RSVP NUMBER IN PARTY:	☐ RSVP NUMBER IN PARTY:
NAME:	NAME:
ADDRESS:	ADDRESS:
PHONE:	PHONE:
EMAIL:	EMAIL:
☐ RSVP NUMBER IN PARTY:	☐ RSVP NUMBER IN PARTY:
NAME:	NAME:
ADDRESS:	ADDRESS:
PHONE:	PHONE:
EMAIL:	EMAIL:
☐ RSVP NUMBER IN PARTY:	☐ RSVP NUMBER IN PARTY:

6

NAME:	NAME:
ADDRESS:	ADDRESS:
PHONE:	PHONE:
EMAIL:	EMAIL:
☐ RSVP NUMBER IN PARTY:	☐ RSVP NUMBER IN PARTY:
NAME:	NAME:
ADDRESS:	ADDRESS:
PHONE:	PHONE:
EMAIL:	EMAIL:
☐ RSVP NUMBER IN PARTY:	☐ RSVP NUMBER IN PARTY:
NAME:	NAME:
ADDRESS:	ADDRESS:
PHONE:	PHONE:
EMAIL:	EMAIL:
☐ RSVP NUMBER IN PARTY:	☐ RSVP NUMBER IN PARTY:
NAME:	NAME:
ADDRESS:	ADDRESS:
PHONE:	PHONE:
EMAIL:	EMAIL:
☐ RSVP NUMBER IN PARTY:	☐ RSVP NUMBER IN PARTY:
NAME:	NAME:
ADDRESS:	ADDRESS:
PHONE:	PHONE:
EMAIL:	EMAIL:
☐ RSVP NUMBER IN PARTY:	☐ RSVP NUMBER IN PARTY:

6

NAME:	NAME:
ADDRESS:	ADDRESS:
PHONE:	PHONE:
EMAIL:	EMAIL:
☐ RSVP NUMBER IN PARTY:	☐ RSVP NUMBER IN PARTY:
NAME:	NAME:
ADDRESS:	ADDRESS:
PHONE:	PHONE:
EMAIL:	EMAIL:
☐ RSVP NUMBER IN PARTY:	☐ RSVP NUMBER IN PARTY:
NAME:	NAME:
ADDRESS:	ADDRESS:
PHONE:	PHONE:
EMAIL:	EMAIL:
☐ RSVP NUMBER IN PARTY:	☐ RSVP NUMBER IN PARTY:
NAME:	NAME:
ADDRESS:	ADDRESS:
PHONE:	PHONE:
EMAIL:	EMAIL:
☐ RSVP NUMBER IN PARTY:	☐ RSVP NUMBER IN PARTY:
NAME:	NAME:
ADDRESS:	ADDRESS:
PHONE:	PHONE:
EMAIL:	EMAIL:
☐ RSVP NUMBER IN PARTY:	☐ RSVP NUMBER IN PARTY:

6

KEEPING TRACK OF GIFTS

During the gift-opening part of the shower, put someone you trust (an organized bridesmaid, your mother, a friend—not your six-year-old niece) in charge of noting each gift and who gave it. Make sure the person charged with keeping track of the gifts understands the importance of the task. Choose someone who can stay focused even if things get hectic, so when you write your thank-you notes, you won't thank someone for the wrong gift or, worse, forget to thank someone altogether.

NAME	DESCRIPTION OF GIFT	THANK-YOU NOTE SENT?
BRIDAL SHOWER GIFT RECORDER		
		☐
		☐
		☐
		☐
		☐
		☐
		☐
		☐
		☐
		☐
		☐

NAME	DESCRIPTION OF GIFT	THANK-YOU NOTE SENT?
		☐
		☐
		☐
		☐
		☐
		☐
		☐
		☐
		☐
		☐
		☐
		☐
		☐
		☐
		☐
		☐

BRIDAL SHOWER GIFT RECORDER (CONTINUED)

NAME	DESCRIPTION OF GIFT	THANK-YOU NOTE SENT?
		☐
		☐
		☐
		☐
		☐
		☐
		☐
		☐
		☐
		☐
		☐
		☐
		☐
		☐
		☐

6

THE BACHELORETTE AND BACHELOR PARTIES

Bachelorette and bachelor parties are usually held a month or two before the wedding. These fun-filled, sometimes over-the-top events are a great way to bond with your closest friends and family members. It's a time to celebrate the fun memories of your single life while looking forward to your upcoming marriage. Parties can range from a quiet restaurant dinner close to home or an afternoon of crafting or antiquing, to an all-night bar crawl or three-day blowout at a beach resort or casino hotel. However you decide to celebrate, take time to honor and appreciate your friends and relatives and the life you've all shared to this point. While these parties are typically split up by gender, you and your fiancé could combine crews and throw an all-inclusive bash.

6

BACHELORETTE PARTY GUEST LIST WORKSHEET

NAME:	NAME:
ADDRESS:	ADDRESS:
PHONE:	PHONE:
EMAIL:	EMAIL:
☐ RSVP	☐ RSVP
NAME:	NAME:
ADDRESS:	ADDRESS:
PHONE:	PHONE:
EMAIL:	EMAIL:
☐ RSVP	☐ RSVP
NAME:	NAME:
ADDRESS:	ADDRESS:
PHONE:	PHONE:
EMAIL:	EMAIL:
☐ RSVP	☐ RSVP
NAME:	NAME:
ADDRESS:	ADDRESS:
PHONE:	PHONE:
EMAIL:	EMAIL:
☐ RSVP	☐ RSVP
NAME:	NAME:
ADDRESS:	ADDRESS:
PHONE:	PHONE:
EMAIL:	EMAIL:
☐ RSVP	☐ RSVP

6

BACHELOR PARTY GUEST LIST WORKSHEET

NAME:	NAME:
ADDRESS:	ADDRESS:
PHONE:	PHONE:
EMAIL:	EMAIL:
☐ RSVP	☐ RSVP
NAME:	NAME:
ADDRESS:	ADDRESS:
PHONE:	PHONE:
EMAIL:	EMAIL:
☐ RSVP	☐ RSVP
NAME:	NAME:
ADDRESS:	ADDRESS:
PHONE:	PHONE:
EMAIL:	EMAIL:
☐ RSVP	☐ RSVP
NAME:	NAME:
ADDRESS:	ADDRESS:
PHONE:	PHONE:
EMAIL:	EMAIL:
☐ RSVP	☐ RSVP
NAME:	NAME:
ADDRESS:	ADDRESS:
PHONE:	PHONE:
EMAIL:	EMAIL:
☐ RSVP	☐ RSVP

6

ATTENDANTS' PARTY

An attendants' party gives you the chance to turn the tables—to honor the people who've been honoring (and assisting) you. Usually, this party is scheduled a week or two before the wedding. It gives everyone a chance to relax, and gives you the opportunity to thank them for all they have done for you during this busy time.

This may be the perfect time to give your attendants the gifts you've bought for them (though if you want to wait until the rehearsal dinner, that's fine too). The guest list does not have to be limited to the attendants; family and close friends can also be included. To keep the atmosphere relaxed, consider having a barbecue, a park picnic, or a day at the beach. You might also want to consider taking a hiatus from wedding talk. Make it a day (or night) to concentrate on what's going on in your attendants' lives. You may have been missing out on some good stuff while you were caught up in your own wedding whirlwind.

6

ATTENDANTS' PARTY WORKSHEET

LOCATION:

PHONE: EMAIL:

CONTACT:

DATE: TIME:

NUMBER OF GUESTS:

MENU

BEVERAGES

ACTIVITIES

OTHER

COST

TOTAL AMOUNT DUE: $

NOTES

CHAPTER 7

The Ceremony

Deciding on the details of your wedding ceremony should be one of your first priorities. If you don't know the location, date, and time of your ceremony, then you can't do much of the reception planning. You'll first need to decide whether you prefer a religious or civil ceremony. If you are interested in having a religious ceremony, consult with your officiant as soon as possible about the availability of the ceremony location for the date you've selected. You will also want to know of any restrictions and guidelines that will apply.

Civil ceremonies are usually quite a bit easier to pull together than a ceremony in a house of worship. Civil ceremonies can be held at city hall or a courthouse, but they are usually held at the reception site, which tends to make things more convenient for all involved. The party simply moves from one area of the ballroom or country club to another after the vows are recited.

RELIGIOUS CEREMONIES

If you decide to have a religious ceremony, consult with your officiant about premarital requirements as soon as you can. You want to make sure you and the religious organization are on the same wavelength regarding these important issues:

- What are the requirements (including any premarital counseling) for getting married?

- Are interfaith ceremonies permitted? What are the requirements or restrictions involved?

- Is the date (and time) you're interested in available?

- Who will perform the ceremony?

- Are visiting clergy allowed to take part in the ceremony?

- Are there any restrictions on decorations? On music?

- Is another wedding scheduled for the same day as yours?

- Are there any restrictions on where the photographer and videographer can stand (or move) during the ceremony? Is flash photography allowed?

- Will you be allowed to hold a receiving line on-site (in the back of the church or synagogue or in a courtyard)?

You should also ask about the cost of the ceremony and the use of church (or synagogue, mosque, etc.) personnel and facilities. This payment is typically referred to as a donation. It doesn't go to any single individual but to the religious organization as a whole.

OFFICIANT WORKSHEET

OFFICIANT/CLERGY NAME:

ADDRESS:

PHONE: EMAIL:

FIRST MEETING

DATE: TIME:

LOCATION:

NOTES

SECOND MEETING

DATE: TIME:

LOCATION:

NOTES

Your first meeting with the officiant should clear up most of the technical details and allow you to ask questions. After everything is settled, the way will be clear for you to personalize the ceremony with music, readings, special prayers, and even your own vows.

CIVIL CEREMONIES

Civil ceremonies are typically performed by a justice of the peace. But if you'd like a personalized ceremony, there's another option. Some couples turn to a friend or family member, asking them to become online ordained ministers. If you think about it, it makes sense: Online ordination is a fairly simple process—in many cases, it's free, and it does make for a very personal ceremony. One caveat: Check the marriage laws in your state. If a minister has to be affiliated with a brick-and-mortar church in order to perform marriages, you'll either have to go the more traditional route...or move your wedding to a location that's more hospitable to modern ministry!

For more information on online ordination, check out these websites:

- www.themonastery.org
- www.amfellow.org
- www.spiritualhumanism.org

CEREMONY PLANNING WORKSHEET

LOCATION:

ADDRESS:

DATE: TIME:

OFFICIANT'S NAME:

COST

LOCATION FEE: $

OFFICIANT'S FEE: $

REC. DONATION: $

PART OF CEREMONY

- ☐ Processional
- ☐ Opening words
- ☐ Giving away
- ☐ Reading
- ☐ Prayers
- ☐ Marriage vows

- ☐ Exchanging of rings
- ☐ Pronouncement of marriage
- ☐ Closing words
- ☐ Recessional
- ☐ Other:
- ☐ Other:

Wedding program available?   ☐ Yes   ☐ No

NOTES

7

WRITING YOUR OWN VOWS

Whether you have a religious or civil ceremony, your officiant can provide you with the standard wedding vows. But writing your own will make them a personal and meaningful part of your wedding ceremony. If you'd like to try writing your own vows, here are some tips to help make them heartfelt and memorable:

- Think about your journey as a couple, your shared experiences, and what makes your love unique. What do you love most about your partner? What are your hopes and dreams for your future together?

- Decide on the tone of your vows. They can be romantic, sentimental, humorous, or a mix of these. Make sure your tone reflects your personalities and the overall atmosphere of the wedding.

- Share personal stories, inside jokes, or significant moments from your relationship. This will make your vows more relatable and engaging for your guests.

- Think about what you're committing to, such as love, support, and partnership. Be specific and clear in your promises.

- While your vows are deeply personal, remember that you're sharing them with your family and friends. Make sure they are comfortable for all to hear and don't include anything that might embarrass or offend anyone.

- Aim for your vows to be around one to two minutes each. This keeps them meaningful without making them too long.

When it's time to deliver your vows, focus on your partner and the significance of the moment. Don't worry too much about the audience; it's a special moment between the two of you.

ANSWER TOGETHER

How do you, as a couple, define the following terms?

Love:	Trust:
Marriage:	Family:
Commitment:	Togetherness:

7

How did the two of you first meet?

List any shared hobbies or mutual interests.

What was the single most important event in your relationship?
(Or what is the event that you feel says the most about your
development as a couple?)

How similar (or different) were your respective childhoods? Take a
moment and try to recount some of the important parallels here.

Is there a song, poem, or book that is particularly meaningful in your
relationship? If so, identify it here.

Do you and your partner share a common religious tradition?
If so, identify it here.

Why did your parents' marriages succeed or fail? What marital pitfalls
do you want to avoid? What can you take from your parents' examples,
good or bad?

Take some time to reminisce about the course of your relationship.
When did you first realize you loved each other? When did you first say
the words? What trials and tribulations has your love had to overcome?
What shared memories are you most fond of?

How do you and your partner look at personal growth and change? What
aspects of your life together are likely to change over the coming years?
How do you anticipate dealing with those changes? How important is
mutual respect and tolerance in your relationship? When one of you feels
that a particular need is being overlooked, what do you feel is the best
way to address this problem with the other person?

Do you and your partner have a common vision of what your life will be like as older people? Will it include children or grandchildren? Take this opportunity to put into words the vision you and your partner share of what it will be like to grow old together.

7

ANSWER SEPARATELY

What was the first thing you noticed about your partner?

BRIDE:	GROOM:

What do you love about your partner? Why?

BRIDE:	GROOM:

7

7

CHAPTER 8

The Venue

You're going to spend most of your wedding budget on the reception, so start looking for venues early to book the place you want! First, decide whether you are more particular about the site of the wedding ceremony or the reception. If you just have to be married in the church your parents were married in, for example, and its available dates don't coincide with those of the reception site you're considering, then you'll just have to find another reception location. On the other hand, if you want your reception in a certain location, but the site of the actual ceremony doesn't really matter to you, your choice is obvious.

8

INVESTIGATE THE POSSIBILITIES

You can start your search for the ideal reception site by asking friends and family for their recommendations. Visit the places you're considering and ask tons of questions. Here are some to start with:

- How many people can the facility comfortably seat?

- Does the site have a minimum charge for a reception?

- How many hours is the site available? Is there a minimum amount of time you must reserve? Are there charges if the reception runs over?

- How are weddings typically set up in the space?

- Is in-house catering available? Can you bring in your own caterer?

- If you're opting for food stations, where will they be set up?

- Does the facility provide all you need, or will you have to rent tables, chairs, linens, china, glassware, or other items?

- How many restrooms will be available for your guests?

- If the reception is to be held outdoors, what is the venue's inclement weather policy?

- If there isn't a bar, where can your caterer set up their bar?

- If you've arranged for an open bar, are there any limits as to what kinds of alcohol will be served? If you've arranged for a cash bar, what will the prices be?

- Is there a separate area for cocktails?

- How big is the dance floor?

- Where will the band or DJ set up?

- Is there free parking? If there is valet parking, what are the rates and gratuities?

- Is there a private area for the wedding party to use before and during the reception?

○ Does the facility have more than one reception room on the premises? Is yours the only reception scheduled that day, or is there one before or after?

○ What are the cancellation policies? Is the deposit refundable?

Of course, you'll probably have many other questions of your own. Be sure to take some time before each meeting to read through the Venue Questions Worksheet later in this chapter and add your specific questions.

VENUE COSTS

Make sure you're aware of all reception-related charges up front. A deposit will reserve the site you want. Many sites won't refund this deposit if you decide you don't want to use the facility. Before you sign on the dotted line, get references and review the agreement carefully. As always, make sure every part of your final negotiations, including date, time, services, and policies, is in writing.

8

How many people can the facility comfortably seat?

How many hours is the site available?

Is there a minimum amount of time I must reserve? Are there charges if the reception runs over?

8

How are weddings typically set up in the space? Will I be able to suggest a different setup?

Is in-house catering available? Can I bring in my own caterer?

If I opt for food stations, where would they be set up?

Does the facility provide all I need, or will I have to rent tables, chairs, linens, china, glassware, or other items?

If the reception is held outdoors, what is your inclement weather policy?

Is there a bar? If not, where can my caterer set one up?

Are there any limits as to what kinds of alcohol will be served for an open bar?

8

What would prices be for a cash bar?

Is there a separate area for cocktails?

How big is the dance floor?

Where will the band or DJ set up?

Where will guests park? Is there a fee for parking?

If there is valet parking, what are the rates?

Is there a private area for the wedding party to use before and during the reception?

How many restrooms will be available for guests?

8

Do you have more than one reception room on the premises? Will ours be the only reception scheduled that day?

What are the cancellation policies? Is the deposit refundable?

Other questions:

RECEPTION SITE WORKSHEET

RECEPTION SITE (OPTION 1)

NAME OF SITE:

ADDRESS:

WEBSITE:

PHONE: EMAIL:

CONTACT:

APPOINTMENTS

DATE: TIME: DATE: TIME:

DATE: TIME: DATE: TIME:

LOCATION INFORMATION

DATE: TIME:

OCCUPANCY:

FINAL HEAD COUNT DUE DATE:

NUMBER OF HOURS:

OVERTIME COST: $

LOCATION INCLUDES THE FOLLOWING

SERVICES: EQUIPMENT:

COST

TOTAL AMOUNT DUE: $

AMOUNT OF DEPOSIT: $ DATE:

BALANCE DUE: $ DATE:

TERMS OF CANCELLATION

NOTES

8

RECEPTION COSTS (OPTION 1)

ITEM	DESCRIPTION/NOTES	COST
SITE RENTAL		
OVERTIME FEE:		$
OTHER:		$
EQUIPMENT		
TENT:		$
CHAIRS:		$
TABLES:		$
LINENS:		$
OTHER:		$
SERVICE		
SERVERS:		$
BARTENDERS:		$
VALET PARKING ATTENDANTS:		$
COAT CHECKERS:		$
OTHER		
		$
		$
		$
		$
Total:		$

RECEPTION SITE (OPTION 2)

NAME OF SITE:

ADDRESS:

WEBSITE:

PHONE: EMAIL:

CONTACT:

APPOINTMENTS

DATE: TIME: DATE: TIME:

DATE: TIME: DATE: TIME:

LOCATION INFORMATION

DATE: TIME:

OCCUPANCY:

FINAL HEAD COUNT DUE DATE:

NUMBER OF HOURS:

OVERTIME COST: $

LOCATION INCLUDES THE FOLLOWING

SERVICES: EQUIPMENT:

COST

TOTAL AMOUNT DUE: $

AMOUNT OF DEPOSIT: $ DATE:

BALANCE DUE: $ DATE:

TERMS OF CANCELLATION

NOTES

RECEPTION SITE WORKSHEET (CONTINUED)

RECEPTION COSTS (OPTION 2)

ITEM	DESCRIPTION/NOTES	COST
SITE RENTAL		
OVERTIME FEE:		$
OTHER:		$
EQUIPMENT		
TENT:		$
CHAIRS:		$
TABLES:		$
LINENS:		$
OTHER:		$
SERVICE		
SERVERS:		$
BARTENDERS:		$
VALET PARKING ATTENDANTS:		$
COAT CHECKERS:		$
OTHER		
		$
		$
		$
		$
Total:		$

8

CHAPTER 9

The Reception Timeline

Your wedding reception will be unique to you and your partner's tastes, preferences, and budget, but one thing all receptions need is a structured timeline. Creating a wedding reception timeline can help ensure that the event runs smoothly and all important moments are captured. Here's a sample plan for a traditional evening wedding celebration, with a cocktail hour and a four-hour reception. Keep in mind that this is just a general template. Use it as a guide to create your own dream wedding timeline.

9

5:00 PM		
5:15 PM	5:00–6:00 PM **COCKTAIL HOUR**	Guests arrive, mingle, and enjoy cocktails and appetizers. Live music or background music can enhance the atmosphere.
5:30 PM		
5:45 PM		
6:00 PM	6:00–6:15 PM **GUESTS ENTER RECEPTION**	Guests will be asked to find their seats and get ready for the entrance of the wedding party.
6:15 PM	6:15–6:25 PM **GRAND ENTRANCE**	The bridal party and newlyweds are introduced as they enter the reception venue.
	6:25–6:35 PM **FIRST DANCE**	The newlyweds share their first dance as a married couple.
6:30 PM	6:35–6:45 PM **WELCOME SPEECH AND/OR BLESSING**	You may want to have your officiant or a family friend offer a blessing. The dinner is usually kicked off by a toast, usually from the parents or father of the bride.
6:45 PM	6:45–7:00 PM **FIRST COURSE**	As soon as the toasts end, the waitstaff will serve the first course.
7:00 PM	7:00–7:20 PM **MAID OF HONOR AND BEST MAN SPEECHES**	Usually, the maid of honor goes first. Other guests may offer a toast as well.
7:15 PM		
7:30 PM	7:20–7:45 PM **MAIN COURSE**	The band or DJ will play background music during dinner. If you're having a buffet dinner, the DJ or emcee will let each table know when to head to the buffet tables.

9

7:45 PM	**7:45–8:00 PM** **PARENT DANCES**	This is the time for the father-daughter dance, mother-son dance, or any other special dances.
8:00 PM		
8:15 PM		The DJ or live band will play music for guests to dance. Start with a high-energy favorite to get everyone out there. Break up the dancing with the bouquet toss and garter toss if you're doing them.
8:30 PM		
8:45 PM		
9:00 PM	**8:00–10:30 PM** **DANCING**	
9:15 PM		

9:30–9:40 PM

CAKE CUTTING

The newlyweds cut the cake,
and dessert is served.

9:30 PM

9

9:50–11:00 PM

LAST DANCE & GOODBYES

9:45 PM

10:00 PM

End your wedding with a favorite song

10:15 PM

before you say goodbye to your guests

10:30 PM

(or head to the after-party).

10:45 PM

Your guests will be ushered toward
the exit to send you off with confetti,
sparklers, or bubbles or to just wave
and wish you well.

11:00 PM

11:00 PM
SEND-OFF

RECEPTION EVENTS WORKSHEET

BRIDAL PARTY ENTRANCE

INTRODUCE ENTIRE BRIDAL PARTY? ☐ Yes ☐ No

MUSIC:

INTRODUCE ONLY BRIDE & GROOM? ☐ Yes ☐ No

MUSIC:

FAMILY

PARENT(S) OF BRIDE:	PARENT(S) OF GROOM:
GRANDPARENT(S) OF BRIDE:	GRANDPARENT(S) OF GROOM:

ATTENDANTS

FLOWER GIRL(S):	RING BEARER(S):
BRIDESMAIDS:	USHERS:
MAID OF HONOR:	BEST MAN:

MATRON OF HONOR:

BRIDE'S FIRST NAME:	GROOM'S FIRST NAME:

BRIDE AND GROOM AS THEY ARE TO BE INTRODUCED

RECEPTION EVENTS WORKSHEET (CONTINUED)

AFTER BRIDAL ENTRANCE

RECEIVING LINE AT RECEPTION? ☐ Yes ☐ No

WHEN:

MUSIC:

BLESSING? ☐ Yes ☐ No

BY WHOM:

FIRST TOAST? ☐ Yes ☐ No

BY WHOM:

OTHER TOASTS? ☐ Yes ☐ No

BY WHOM:

BY WHOM:

BY WHOM:

SPECIAL DANCES

FIRST DANCE? ☐ Yes ☐ No

WHEN:

MUSIC:

TO JOIN IN FIRST DANCE

MAID OF HONOR AND BEST MAN? ☐ Yes ☐ No

PARENTS OF BRIDE AND GROOM? ☐ Yes ☐ No

BRIDESMAIDS AND USHERS? ☐ Yes ☐ No

GUESTS? ☐ Yes ☐ No

OPEN DANCE FLOOR FOR GUESTS
   AFTER FIRST DANCE? ☐ Yes ☐ No

PARENT DANCES

FATHER-DAUGHTER DANCE? ☐ Yes ☐ No

MUSIC:

MOTHER-SON DANCE? ☐ Yes ☐ No

MUSIC:

9

RECEPTION EVENTS WORKSHEET (CONTINUED)

AFTER DINNER

CAKE CUTTING?	☐ Yes	☐ No
MUSIC:		
BOUQUET TOSS?	☐ Yes	☐ No
GARTER TOSS?	☐ Yes	☐ No
LAST DANCE?	☐ Yes	☐ No
MUSIC:		

OTHER EVENTS

EVENT

WHEN:

MUSIC:

EVENT

WHEN:

MUSIC:

SPECIAL REQUESTS AND DEDICATIONS

NOTES

CHAPTER 10

The Seating Chart

Unless you're planning a cocktail reception with hors d'oeuvres or an informal buffet, you're going to need a seating chart. Guests (especially those who don't know many people at the reception) often feel uncomfortable without assigned seating.

10

PLACING PEOPLE

The easiest way to alert guests to their table assignments is to place table cards on a table near the reception room entrance. Table cards list the name of the guest and their table assignment. Another option is to set up an enlarged seating diagram at the reception entrance.

The head table is wherever the bride and groom sit, and for traditional weddings, it's a long table with the bride and groom in the middle. The best man sits next to the bride and the maid of honor sits next to the groom. The attendants are seated on either side. But that's not the only option. You can sit at a round table with your attendants or choose to have an intimate table for the two of you.

Here are some things to consider as you plan the seating for the rest of the guests:

- **Parents:** The parents of the bride and groom usually sit at separate tables with their own families. Still, there's no single correct seating arrangement for the parents' tables. The bride's and groom's parents can sit together with the officiant, or each set of parents can host their own table with family and friends.

- **Officiant:** The officiant should be seated in a place of honor at the reception. Make sure that one of the parents' tables includes the officiant and his or her spouse.

- **Divorced Parents:** Where you seat divorced parents will depend on the quality of their relationship. If they're cordial and used to spending time together at family functions, you may want to seat exes at the same table. But if they don't get along, set them up at tables that are equally distant from the head table while being as far apart from each other as possible.

- **The Rest of the Guests:** Seat people who know each other together. Of course, you'll seat members of each family together, but you should also group friends according to their relationships with each other (for example, college friends, your work colleagues, hometown neighbors).

SEATING CHART WORKSHEET

HEAD TABLE

SHAPE OF TABLE: NUMBER OF CHAIRS:

ORDER OF SEATING (LIST OR DRAW DIAGRAM HERE):

BRIDE'S PARENTS' TABLE

SHAPE OF TABLE: NUMBER OF CHAIRS:

ORDER OF SEATING (LIST OR DRAW DIAGRAM HERE):

10

GROOM'S PARENTS' TABLE

SHAPE OF TABLE: NUMBER OF CHAIRS:

ORDER OF SEATING (LIST OR DRAW DIAGRAM HERE):

GUEST TABLES

SHAPE OF TABLES:

AVERAGE NUMBER OF CHAIRS PER TABLE:

TOTAL NUMBER OF GUESTS:

TABLE NUMBER:	**TABLE NUMBER:**
NAME OF GUEST:	NAME OF GUEST:
TABLE NUMBER:	**TABLE NUMBER:**
NAME OF GUEST:	NAME OF GUEST:
TABLE NUMBER:	**TABLE NUMBER:**
NAME OF GUEST:	NAME OF GUEST:
TABLE NUMBER:	**TABLE NUMBER:**
NAME OF GUEST:	NAME OF GUEST:

10

TABLE NUMBER:

NAME OF GUEST:

TABLE NUMBER:

NAME OF GUEST:

TABLE NUMBER:

NAME OF GUEST:

TABLE NUMBER:

NAME OF GUEST:

TABLE NUMBER:

NAME OF GUEST:

TABLE NUMBER:

NAME OF GUEST:

10

TABLE NUMBER:

NAME OF GUEST:

TABLE NUMBER:

NAME OF GUEST:

TABLE NUMBER:

NAME OF GUEST:

TABLE NUMBER:

NAME OF GUEST:

TABLE NUMBER:

NAME OF GUEST:

TABLE NUMBER:

NAME OF GUEST:

TABLE NUMBER:

NAME OF GUEST:

TABLE NUMBER:

NAME OF GUEST:

TABLE NUMBER:

NAME OF GUEST:

TABLE NUMBER:

NAME OF GUEST:

10

CHAPTER 11

The Food and the Cake

Along with your budget, the type and location of your reception will help you determine the kind of caterer you need. After that, all that's left is to find out who can best feed your guests at a price you can afford.

11

IN-HOUSE CATERERS

If you're lucky, your reception site will have an in-house caterer who fits your budget, serves great food, and knows how to work with you. There are several advantages to using an in-house caterer, the biggest being that you don't have to go to the trouble of finding one yourself. They are already familiar with the particulars of the room, which itself is a perk with many advantages. For instance, linens and dinnerware that complement the overall atmosphere are already in rotation, and the waitstaff have already carefully choreographed their serving routine.

In-house catering is usually more expensive than independent catering, often charging you for lots of little extras (things you may not want or need) as part of one all-inclusive package. However, if the food is good and the price is just a little on the high side, you might find that this arrangement is worth the money simply because it's so convenient.

INDEPENDENT CATERERS

Finding an independent food-and-drink team is actually fairly easy. The good ones sell themselves by word of mouth (ask any business manager or event planner or even a friend who entertains regularly for their recommendations), and there are always fresh upstarts in this business who are eager to show off their wares.

Before you go searching for an independent caterer, find out what your reception site provides and what it doesn't. Some sites offer linens, glass- and dinnerware, tables, chairs—everything but the food. Others provide nothing but the space. Know what you'll need before you look for a caterer.

Bare-bones caterers specialize in keeping it simple. They provide food, and that's it. Everything else—beverages, linens, dinnerware, glasses, even servers—is left completely up to you. Sometimes, this can work to your advantage. These types of caterers may offer great food at a low price, and you may be able to find a good deal on everything else that you'll need. You can save quite a bit of money this way. If you purchase alcohol in quantity, for instance, you'll avoid the markups that usually accompany liquor provided by caterers.

The disadvantage, of course, is the inconvenience. If your reception site doesn't provide tables and chairs, for example, you'll have to research what you'll need and determine a fair price for the cost of any rentals. Then you'll have to orchestrate getting everything to the site on your wedding day and returning it. The task is not impossible, but it may require more work than you initially think, and during a very busy time to boot.

Full-service caterers, which most people associate with a wedding reception, provide food, beverages, waitstaff, and bartenders. Most also offer linens and dinnerware. If you need tables and chairs, these caterers will usually do all the legwork for you and simply add that to your bill. Be sure to get a written estimate before you authorize anything.

One last tip: Even if you ask for recommendations from friends, relatives, and business associates, don't hire a caterer until you have sampled the food you plan on serving to your guests. Any caterer worth their salt will offer you a chance to try samples, so don't hesitate to ask.

QUESTIONS TO ASK THE CATERER

No matter what type of caterer you choose, you'll need to ask a lot of questions to make sure they can provide the services you're looking for.

THE COST

Caterers can give you an estimate based on current food prices. Closer to the wedding, they should be able to give you the final price, reflecting the prices at that time. Ask about how much of a difference you should expect and if they offer price guarantees. Here are some other questions to ask:

○ Does the overall estimate include meals for the photographer, videographer, DJ or band, and anyone else who will be working for you that day?

○ Does the cost cover gratuities for the staff and the cost of the bartender, coatroom attendant, and anyone else who will be working at your reception?

○ What is the refund policy?

THE FOOD

No matter how simple or fancy the service, you want to know whether this caterer can meet your needs. Ask:

○ What are the options for appetizers during the cocktail hour?

○ Do you provide options for the entrée? Are vegan or kosher meals available if needed? Can you accommodate special diets, like gluten-free or nut-free?

○ Do you provide sit-down, buffet, or station options? What are the price differences? How does each option work?

○ Do you provide a wedding cake? What are the other options for dessert?

○ Can a tasting be arranged? What is the cost of a tasting?

○ What happens to leftover food?

THE CONTRACT

When you decide on a caterer who meets your budget and who has answered your questions to your satisfaction, get every part of your agreement in writing. If you're not familiar with a caterer's work, or if they are new to the business, ask for references. This is critically important when you're planning almost a year ahead. You'll be asked to give a sizable deposit, and you want to make sure the caterer will still be in business when the date arrives!

CATERER WORKSHEET

CATERER (OPTION 1)

NAME:

ADDRESS:

PHONE: _____ EMAIL:

CONTACT: _____ HOURS:

APPOINTMENTS

DATE: _____ TIME: _____ | DATE: _____ TIME: _____

DATE: _____ TIME: _____ | DATE: _____ TIME: _____

PACKAGE INFORMATION

DATE OF HIRED SERVICES: _____ TIME:

NUMBER OF HOURS: _____ COCKTAIL HOUR: ☐ Yes ☐ No

MENU

☐ Sit Down ☐ Buffet

CATERER INCLUDES THE FOLLOWING

SERVICES: _____ EQUIPMENT:

COST

TOTAL AMOUNT DUE: $

AMOUNT OF DEPOSIT: $ _____ DATE:

BALANCE DUE: $ _____ DATE:

GRATUITIES INCLUDED? ☐ Yes ☐ No

SALES TAX INCLUDED? ☐ Yes ☐ No

TERMS OF CANCELLATION | **NOTES**

CATERER COSTS (OPTION 1)

ITEM	DESCRIPTION/NOTES	COST
FOOD		
APPETIZERS		$
ENTRÉES		$
DESSERT		$
OTHER FOOD		$
BEVERAGES		
NONALCOHOLIC		$
CHAMPAGNE/WINE		$
LIQUOR		$
EQUIPMENT		
TENT		$
CHAIRS		$
TABLES		$
LINENS		$
DINNERWARE		$
FLATWARE		$
GLASSWARE		$
SERVING PIECES		$
SERVICE		
SERVERS		$
BARTENDERS		$
PARKING ATTENDANTS		$
COAT CHECKERS		$
OVERTIME COST		$
OTHER		
		$
GRATUITIES		$
SALES TAX		$
Total:		$

CATERER (OPTION 2)

NAME:

ADDRESS:

PHONE: EMAIL:

CONTACT: HOURS:

APPOINTMENTS

DATE: TIME: DATE: TIME:

DATE: TIME: DATE: TIME:

PACKAGE INFORMATION

DATE OF HIRED SERVICES: TIME:

NUMBER OF HOURS: COCKTAIL HOUR: ☐ Yes   ☐ No

MENU

☐ Sit Down   ☐ Buffet

11

CATERER INCLUDES THE FOLLOWING

SERVICES: EQUIPMENT:

COST

TOTAL AMOUNT DUE: $

AMOUNT OF DEPOSIT: $ DATE:

BALANCE DUE: $ DATE:

GRATUITIES INCLUDED?   ☐ Yes   ☐ No

SALES TAX INCLUDED?   ☐ Yes   ☐ No

TERMS OF CANCELLATION   **NOTES**

CATERER WORKSHEET (CONTINUED)

CATERER COSTS (OPTION 2)

ITEM	DESCRIPTION/NOTES	COST
FOOD		
APPETIZERS		$
ENTRÉES		$
DESSERT		$
OTHER FOOD		$
BEVERAGES		
NONALCOHOLIC		$
CHAMPAGNE/WINE		$
LIQUOR		$
EQUIPMENT		
TENT		$
CHAIRS		$
TABLES		$
LINENS		$
DINNERWARE		$
FLATWARE		$
GLASSWARE		$
SERVING PIECES		$
SERVICE		
SERVERS		$
BARTENDERS		$
PARKING ATTENDANTS		$
COAT CHECKERS		$
OVERTIME COST		$
OTHER		
		$
GRATUITIES		$
SALES TAX		$
Total:		**$**

CASH OR OPEN BAR?

One of the hottest topics surrounding any wedding is whether to host a cash bar or an open bar. At the open bar, guests drink for free, courtesy of you or whoever is footing the bill. At a cash bar, they have to pony up for their own drinks. Some people will suggest to you that it's rude to expect your guests to pay for their own drinks. After all, you wouldn't normally host a party and expect your guests to pay for what you serve them.

The other side of the debate is the fact that open bars can end up being extremely expensive. People are often wasteful with liquor that they haven't paid for. Someone might order a drink, take a sip, and go off to the powder room. The drink is forgotten, or the guest assumes it's gotten warm and orders a fresh one. Besides, why shouldn't this guest take full advantage of your generosity?

OTHER OPTIONS

If you really don't want to make your guests buy drinks, there are a few options that might work for you:

- Have an open bar for the first hour of the reception only.

- Serve one or two signature drinks, along with wine and beer.

- Place bottles of wine on the tables to ensure that everyone gets a glass or two with their meal.

- If your reception site allows it, you may be able to save some money by purchasing a few kegs or several cases of high-quality beer plus some cases of good wine. Offer other alcohol or cocktails for cash for those who prefer something stronger.

FOOD AND BEVERAGE WORKSHEET

FOOD	DESCRIPTION/NOTES	NUMBER	COST
APPETIZERS			
			$
			$
			$
ENTRÉES			
			$
			$
			$
			$
DESSERTS (IF ANY)			
			$
			$
BEVERAGES (NONALCOHOLIC)			
			$
			$
WINE/CHAMPAGNE			
			$
			$
OPEN BAR			
			$
			$
			$
OTHER			
			$
			$
GRATUITIES			$
SALES TAX			$
Total:			$

EQUIPMENT RENTAL WORKSHEET

CONTACT INFORMATION

NAME OF RENTAL COMPANY:

ADDRESS:

PHONE: EMAIL:

CONTACT: HOURS:

ORDER DATE:

DELIVERY INFORMATION

☐ Delivery   ☐ Pick Up

DATE: TIME:

SPECIAL INSTRUCTIONS

COST

TOTAL AMOUNT DUE: $

AMOUNT OF DEPOSIT: $ DATE:

BALANCE DUE: $ DATE:

CANCELLATION POLICY

DAMAGED GOODS POLICY

NOTES

11

THE CAKE

Your wedding cake can be as simple or as ornate as you want it to be. It can be one tier or seven. It can be stacked up on its own layers, or it can incorporate architectural supports. And your choices of flavors, fillings, and icings are virtually endless.

There are countless options for decoration. The cake can be garnished with fresh flowers or greenery, and the icing or trimming can be made to match the wedding colors you've selected. The choices for cake flavors, frostings, decorations, and garnishes are plentiful.

Although many couples choose to have a traditional white or yellow cake, chances are you'll be presented with a long, long list of choices: chocolate, chocolate hazelnut, double chocolate, Italian rum, vanilla, lemon, orange, spice, carrot, cheesecake, citron chiffon, fruitcake, banana, Black Forest, cherry—and the list goes on. You can even choose to have a different flavor for each tier of your cake. Cake fillings may include lemon, custard, raspberry, strawberry, almond crème, chocolate fudge, chocolate mocha, chocolate mousse, pineapple, or cherry.

INTERVIEWING BAKERS

Make an appointment to meet with each baker you're considering. You want to make sure you have enough time to ask all your questions and, ideally, to taste a few cakes. And of course, ask for references. If you want your cake to include your wedding colors, bring a swatch of fabric with you. If there's a particular style of cake that you like, bring some photos or sketches. You'll also need to bring along the names and numbers of your florist and photographer as well as all the relevant information regarding your reception site (location, contact name and number, and directions).

Here are some issues to address with the baker:

○ The number of guests

○ Flavor, filling, and icing options

○ The design and structure of the cake

○ Cake decorations

○ When to schedule a cake tasting

○ Costs

○ The groom's cake if you're having one

○ Backup plans for a cake disaster

Your decorated cake does not have to serve all of the guests. You can provide other dessert options along with the cake slices to avoid having an oversized cake. Small pastries, fancy cookies, and cupcakes are all great options to serve alongside the wedding cake.

11

BAKER WORKSHEET

BAKERY (OPTION 1)

CONTACT INFORMATION

NAME OF BAKERY:

WEBSITE:

PHONE: EMAIL:

CONTACT: HOURS:

ORDER DATE:

APPOINTMENTS

DATE: TIME: DATE: TIME:

DATE: TIME: DATE: TIME:

DELIVERY INFORMATION

☐ Delivery   ☐ Pick Up   TIME:

SPECIAL INSTRUCTIONS:

COST

TOTAL AMOUNT DUE: $

AMOUNT OF DEPOSIT: $ DATE:

BALANCE DUE: $ DATE:

SALES TAX INCLUDED?   ☐ Yes   ☐ No

TERMS OF CANCELLATION

NOTES

BAKERY (OPTION 2)

CONTACT INFORMATION

NAME OF BAKERY:

WEBSITE:

PHONE: EMAIL:

CONTACT: HOURS:

ORDER DATE:

APPOINTMENTS

DATE: TIME: DATE: TIME:

DATE: TIME: DATE: TIME:

DELIVERY INFORMATION

☐ Delivery   ☐ Pick Up   TIME:

SPECIAL INSTRUCTIONS:

COST

TOTAL AMOUNT DUE: $

AMOUNT OF DEPOSIT: $ DATE:

BALANCE DUE: $ DATE:

SALES TAX INCLUDED?   ☐ Yes   ☐ No

TERMS OF CANCELLATION

NOTES

11

WEDDING CAKE WORKSHEET

ITEM	DESCRIPTION	COST
WEDDING CAKE		
SIZE		$
SHAPE		$
NUMBER OF TIERS		$
CAKE SERVINGS		$
FLAVOR OF CAKE		$
FLAVOR OF FILLING		$
ICING DECORATIONS		$
FLORAL DECORATIONS		$
GROOM'S CAKE		
SIZE		$
SHAPE		$
CAKE SERVINGS		$
FLAVOR		$
ICING		$
CAKE DECORATIONS		$
OTHER		
		$
		$
		$
DELIVERY CHARGE		$
Total:		$

NOTES

CHAPTER 12

The Invitation

Although most of the people you'll invite to your wedding will probably already know the date, time, and place, you still need to send out invitations. These can be as informal or formal as you like—from a single printed card to a multipart, hand-lettered work of art. Look online for inspiration for invitation designs until you find something you like. Once you have your preferred invitation style, an etiquette guide will provide you with examples of wording to use inside and how to address the outer and inner envelopes.

12

CHOOSING INVITATIONS

Many couples still find their invitations by going to a designated stationery store and browsing through the catalogs. These catalogs contain samples of predesigned invitations—the paper color, paper stock, borders, and ornamentation have already been set. You pick out the color of the paper and ink, the style of the script, and the words you want to use. Many invitations come complete with phrasing. All you do is supply the specific information for your wedding, and the manufacturer does the rest.

You can find countless websites selling traditional and unique invitations. Your best bet is to find one that will send you physical samples so you can feel the quality of the paper stock and raised lettering and get a better idea of ink colors. Don't forget to check the reviews as well. Ordering online invitations is an excellent way to create personalized and inexpensive invitations. And most orders can be processed within a week, so if you're short on time, this may be your best option.

If you can't find an invitation you like online or in a stationery store, or if you want something very specific, there are private printers who can do the job for you. They may be a bit harder to find and more expensive than the big guys, but if you want your invitations to feature embossed lions on roller skates (hey, they're your invitations), private stationers might be your best bet. Look for local printers online.

INVITATION WORDING WORKSHEET

WEDDING INVITATIONS

RETURN ADDRESS FOR INVITATION ENVELOPES

RECEPTION CARDS

RESPONSE CARDS

RETURN ADDRESS FOR RESPONSE CARD ENVELOPES

CEREMONY CARDS

PEW CARDS

RAIN CARDS

12

TRAVEL CARDS

ANNOUNCEMENTS

RETURN ADDRESS FOR ANNOUNCEMENT ENVELOPES

THANK-YOU NOTES

RETURN ADDRESS FOR THANK-YOU NOTE ENVELOPES

CEREMONY PROGRAMS

OTHER

NOTES

12

INVITATION EXTRAS

Most wedding invitations come with outer and inner envelopes, as well as response cards. Depending on the type of wedding you're having, and where, you may need various cards for the entrance to the ceremony, special seating, or weather-related contingencies. You'll need some thank-you notes with both your names on them, and you might want to print some formal announcements.

Ceremony Cards. Ceremony cards guaranteeing entrance into the proceedings are not necessary for a traditional wedding site. However, if your wedding is being held at a public place, such as a museum or a historic mansion, you may need some way to distinguish your guests from the visitors.

Pew Cards. Also called "Within the Ribbon" cards, pew cards can be used if you wish to reserve seats at the ceremony for any special family members or friends. Your guests pass the pew cards to the groomsmen at the ceremony, who will seat the special guests in the front sections marked off as "Reserved."

Plan B. If there's a chance the ceremony or reception could be disrupted or moved due to inclement weather, have cards printed up stating your exact Plan B.

Thank-You Notes. You can order thank-you notes that match your invitations, or you can choose something completely different. The note cards can be as formal or informal as you like. If you already have personal stationery, you might consider using that for your thank-you notes instead of ordering something new.

○ **Announcements.** Many couples are not able to invite everyone on their original guest list. Business associates, friends and family members living far away, and others may have been squeezed off the list due to budget or space constraints. Wedding announcements, sent immediately after the wedding, are a convenient way to let people know of your recent nuptials. They are not sent to anyone who received an invitation.

WHEN TO ORDER

Order your invitations three to four months before the wedding, and always order more than you need. Ordering at least twenty extra invitations will ease the stress among those writing them out and will also save you from having to place a second order. Even if you don't make any mistakes, you'll probably want to have a few invitations as keepsakes anyway.

Be sure to leave yourself plenty of time to address and stamp all of those envelopes. If you're planning a wedding near a holiday, mail out your invitations a few weeks earlier to give your guests some extra time to plan. If you plan to invite more guests as regrets come in, send your invitations out at least eight weeks in advance, with a response date of at least three weeks before the wedding.

12

WEDDING INVITATIONS

DESCRIPTION

MANUFACTURER/WEBSITE/STORE:

STYLE:

PAPER: PAPER COLOR:

TYPEFACE: INK COLOR:

PRINTING PROCESS

INVITATION EXTRAS

TISSUE PAPER INSERTS:	☐ Yes	☐ No
PRINTED OUTER ENVELOPES:	☐ Yes	☐ No
INNER ENVELOPES:	☐ Yes	☐ No COLOR:
ENVELOPE LINER:	☐ Yes	☐ No COLOR:

NUMBER ORDERED	COST	$

RECEPTION CARDS

DESCRIPTION

NUMBER ORDERED	COST	$

RESPONSE CARDS

DESCRIPTION

PRINTED ENVELOPES:

ENVELOPE LINER: ☐ Yes   ☐ No   COLOR:

NUMBER ORDERED	COST	$

12

CEREMONY CARDS

DESCRIPTION

NUMBER ORDERED	COST	$

PEW CARDS

DESCRIPTION

NUMBER ORDERED	COST	$

RAIN CARDS

DESCRIPTION

NUMBER ORDERED	COST	$

TRAVEL CARDS/MAPS

DESCRIPTION

NUMBER ORDERED	COST	$

WEDDING ANNOUNCEMENTS

DESCRIPTION

NUMBER ORDERED	COST	$

PRINTED ENVELOPES:

ENVELOPE LINER: ☐ Yes ☐ No COLOR:

NUMBER ORDERED	COST	$

12

CEREMONY PROGRAMS

DESCRIPTION

NUMBER ORDERED	**COST**	$

THANK-YOU NOTES

DESCRIPTION

PRINTED ENVELOPES:

ENVELOPE LINER: ☐ Yes   ☐ No   COLOR:

NUMBER ORDERED	**COST**	$

OTHER

DESCRIPTION

NUMBER ORDERED	**COST**	$

DESCRIPTION

NUMBER ORDERED	**COST**	$

ORDER INFORMATION

ORDER DATE:

READY DATE: TIME:

DELIVERY/PICK UP INSTRUCTIONS

☐ Delivery   ☐ Pick Up

DATE: TIME:

SPECIAL INSTRUCTIONS:

12

INVITATION WORKSHEET (CONTINUED)

COST

TOTAL AMOUNT DUE: $

AMOUNT OF DEPOSIT: $ DATE:

BALANCE DUE: $ DATE:

SALES TAX INCLUDED?   ☐ Yes   ☐ No

TERMS OF CANCELLATION

NOTES

12

BRIDAL SHOP WORKSHEET

BRIDAL SHOP (OPTION 1)

NAME:

ADDRESS:

CONTACT:

PHONE: EMAIL:

APPOINTMENT 1

DATE: TIME:

NOTES:

APPOINTMENT 2

DATE: TIME:

NOTES:

APPOINTMENT 3

DATE: TIME:

NOTES:

DRESSES

13

BRIDAL SHOP (OPTION 2)

NAME:

ADDRESS:

CONTACT:

PHONE: EMAIL:

APPOINTMENT 1

DATE: TIME:

NOTES:

APPOINTMENT 2

DATE: TIME:

NOTES:

APPOINTMENT 3

DATE: TIME:

NOTES:

13

DRESSES

BRIDE'S ATTIRE WORKSHEET

BRIDAL SALON

NAME OF SALON:

ADDRESS:

PHONE: EMAIL:

CONTACT: STORE HOURS:

NOTES

WEDDING GOWN

DESCRIPTION

MANUFACTURER:

STYLE NUMBER: COLOR:

ORDER DATE: FITTING DATE:

COST

TOTAL AMOUNT DUE: $

AMOUNT OF DEPOSIT: $ DATE:

BALANCE DUE: $ DATE:

SALES TAX INCLUDED?   ☐ Yes   ☐ No

DELIVERY/PICK UP INFORMATION

☐ Delivery   ☐ Pick Up

DATE: TIME:

SPECIAL INSTRUCTIONS:

TERMS OF CANCELLATION | **NOTES**

HEADPIECE AND VEIL

DESCRIPTION

MANUFACTURER:

STYLE NUMBER: COLOR:

IMPORTANT DATES

ORDER DATE: FITTING DATE:

COST

TOTAL AMOUNT DUE: $

AMOUNT OF DEPOSIT: $ DATE:

BALANCE DUE: $ DATE:

SALES TAX INCLUDED?   ☐ Yes   ☐ No

DELIVERY/PICK UP INFORMATION

☐ Delivery   ☐ Pick Up

DATE: TIME:

SPECIAL INSTRUCTIONS:

NOTES

BRIDAL ACCESSORIES COST

ITEM	DESCRIPTION	COST	PICKED UP?
BRA/SLIP:		$	☐
HOSIERY:		$	☐
GARTER:		$	☐
SHOES:		$	☐
JEWELRY:		$	☐
OTHER:		$	☐

BRIDE'S ATTENDANTS' ATTIRE

Start looking for your attendants' dresses as soon as you finalize the wedding party. The women need to begin the attire process early because their dresses have to be ordered (or made) and altered. When searching for your attendants' gowns, check the formal dress section of a quality department store in your area before you go to a bridal salon. You may find appropriate dresses they can wear again in the future—and at a lower price than salon dresses.

Attendants do not have to troop to the bridal salon as a group for fittings. Once they have ordered their dresses, they can go for alterations at their convenience; just be sure to give them a deadline for getting it all done. If one of your bridesmaids lives far away and can't make it to the fittings, ask your salon about other arrangements. If you can, email or text your bridesmaid a photo of the dress you have in mind and make sure she will feel comfortable wearing it. Then ask her for her measurements so that you can order her dress along with the others. Ask the bridal shop about shipping it directly to her. She can follow up with a local tailor for alterations.

13

BRIDE'S ATTENDANTS' ATTIRE WORKSHEET

PLACE OF PURCHASE

NAME:

ADDRESS:

PHONE: EMAIL:

CONTACT: STORE HOURS:

NOTES

ATTENDANTS' ATTIRE

DESCRIPTION OF DRESS

MANUFACTURER:

STYLE NUMBER: COLOR:

NUMBER ORDERED: SIZES ORDERED:

IMPORTANT DATES

ORDER DATE: FITTING DATE:

COST

COST PER DRESS: $

TOTAL COST OF DRESSES: $

DEPOSIT PAID: $ DATE:

BALANCE DUE: $ DATE:

DELIVERY/PICK UP INFORMATION

☐ Delivery   ☐ Pick Up

DATE: TIME:

SPECIAL INSTRUCTIONS:

13

ALTERATIONS

DESCRIPTION OF ALTERATIONS:

ALTERATIONS FEE (TOTAL): $

ACCESSORIES

DESCRIPTION OF ALTERATIONS:

COST OF ACCESSORIES: $

NOTES

MAID/MATRON OF HONOR

NAME: DRESS SIZE:

IMPORTANT DATES

FITTING DATE #1:   TIME:

FITTING DATE #2:   TIME:

FITTING DATE #3:   TIME:

NOTES

13

WEDDING STYLE ON A BUDGET

There is nothing more exciting than your first foray into the bridal shop world. The dresses! The personal service! The champagne! The price tags! And that's where the excitement ends for many women, who find themselves wondering, "Who would pay $5,000 for a dress you can only wear once?" Fortunately, there are plenty of ways to keep your costs down in this area:

○ **Look at white or off-white bridesmaid dresses.** Many are beautifully designed and can be yours for several hundred dollars instead of several thousand.

○ **Visit consignment shops.** Not all consignment stores carry bridal gowns, but many do. Even if you have to have a secondhand dress altered to fit, it will still cost less than buying one brand-new.

○ **Go online.** Check out eBay or sites that sell pre-owned designer fashions like The RealReal or Poshmark for high-end dresses. Again, the dress plus the price of alterations will come to much less than what you'd spend on a new dress.

○ **Borrow.** If you have a sister, cousin, friend, or other relative who has recently walked down the aisle, she may be willing to lend you her dress, as long as you offer to have it cleaned after the ceremony.

○ **Rent a dress.** You should be able to find local bridal shops that offer gowns for rent as well as for sale. Check out sites like Rent the Runway for large selections of expensive dresses that you might never be able to afford.

○ **Go nontraditional.** Sure, bridal dresses in this country are usually white and formal, but there's no rule that says you have to wear such an outfit. Branch out. Choose a dress or suit that you love and will wear again.

No matter what you choose to wear, make sure that you are comfortable with your decision. It doesn't matter what anyone else thinks. Now go find that inexpensive dress!

ACCESSORIES

You've found the perfect dress, but you still need a veil, a headpiece, and all of the other accessories to complete your ensemble. Here are some items to add to your list:

- **Veil.** Your headpiece and veil should complement the style of your dress. Don't pick something so elaborate that it overpowers you and your dress.

- **Shoes.** While silk or satin shoes in the color of your gown are a classic choice, many brides choose more colorful and fun options. Be sure to choose a pair that you can dance and stand in comfortably—remember, you'll be on your feet for hours.

- **Undergarments.** You'll want undergarments that work specifically with your gown. These may include a strapless or push-up bra, a corset or tummy-flattening brief, and a slip or petticoat.

13

MEN'S ATTIRE

Most likely, the men in your wedding party will be wearing some form of tuxedo or suit. Though every tuxedo carries an air of formality, some are actually dressier than others. To brighten up a plain tuxedo, consider having the groomsmen wear vests and bow ties that match or complement the bridesmaids' dresses.

THE GROOM

As long as a groom knows the basics of the wedding details (how formal, which season, the hour), any formalwear shop will point him and his attendants in the right direction. If you're having a very informal wedding—on a beach or in a park, for instance—your groom may not need a tuxedo at all.

Weddings are basically categorized by their pageantry (things like the setting, your dress, the formality or informality of the reception site), and each style carries its own rules about appropriate apparel. While many grooms opt to purchase a good suit they can wear again (and encourage their groomsmen to do the same), here is the classic breakdown of fashion expectations of the groom:

INFORMAL OR SEMIFORMAL	
DAYTIME	
Dark formal suit (in summer, select a lighter shade and fabric), white dress shirt, dress shoes, and dark socks	
SEMIFORMAL	
EVENING	
Formal suit or dinner jacket with matching trousers (preferably black), white shirt, cummerbund or vest, black bow tie, studs, and cuff links	

FORMAL	
DAYTIME	**EVENING**
Cutaway or stroller jacket in gray or black, white high-collared (wing-collared) shirt, waistcoat (usually gray), striped trousers, striped tie or ascot, studs, and cuff links	Black dinner jacket and trousers, white tuxedo shirt, waistcoat, black four-in-hand tie, cummerbund, and cuff links

VERY FORMAL	
DAYTIME	**EVENING**
Cutaway (black or gray), wing-collared shirt, vest, gray striped trousers, ascot, gloves, and cuff links	Black tailcoat, white piqué shirt, white waistcoat, white bow tie, black trousers, patent leather shoes, studs, and cuff links

13

GROOM'S ATTIRE WORKSHEET

TUXEDO SHOP

NAME:

ADDRESS:

PHONE: EMAIL:

CONTACT: STORE HOURS:

INCLUDED SERVICES

GROOM'S MEASUREMENTS

HEIGHT: WEIGHT:

COAT SIZE: ARM INSEAM:

PANTS WAIST: LENGTH (OUTSEAM):

SHIRT NECK: SLEEVE:

SHOE SIZE: WIDTH:

NOTES

13

GROOM'S ATTIRE

TUXEDO STYLE:

TUXEDO COLOR:

IMPORTANT DATES

ORDER DATE:

FITTING DATE #1:   TIME:

FITTING DATE #2:   TIME:

COST

TOTAL AMOUNT DUE: $

AMOUNT OF DEPOSIT: $ DATE:

BALANCE DUE: $ DATE:

GROOM'S ATTIRE WORKSHEET (CONTINUED)

PICK UP/DROP OFF INFORMATION

PICK UP DATE: PICK UP TIME:

DROP OFF DATE: DROP OFF TIME:

SPECIAL INSTRUCTIONS:

LATE FEE: $

TERMS OF CANCELLATION

GROOM ACCESSORIES COST

ITEM	SIZE	COLOR	COST	PICKED UP?
TIE/ASCOT:			$	☐
CUMMERBUND:			$	☐
POCKET SQUARE:			$	☐
SUSPENDERS:			$	☐
STUDS:			$	☐
CUFF LINKS:			$	☐
FORMAL SOCKS:			$	☐
SHOES:			$	☐
OTHER:			$	☐

13

THE GROOM'S ATTENDANTS

In general, all the groomsmen dress the same as each other, in a style and color that complement the groom's outfit. Many men rent their formalwear. Your best bet is to have the men reserve their attire at least two to three months before the wedding.

Any male attendant who lives out of town should go to a reputable formalwear shop in his area to be measured. Have the groomsman send the measurements to your fiancé so he can reserve the attire with the rest of the group's. Remember to ask the formalwear shop about exact prices, including alterations. Also, inquire about their return policy (including when to return the clothing).

13

BRIDAL BEAUTY

You will be the focus of attention on your wedding day, not to mention the hundreds of photos that will be taken. While you could certainly do your own hair and makeup, you'd probably be more comfortable leaving it to the professionals. Start by talking to your own hair stylist. If they're not trained in wedding hair styling and updos, they can probably recommend someone who is. Many wedding hair stylists work together with makeup artists, and hiring a team can make your wedding day prep go much smoother. Here are some things to think about when planning your pre-wedding beauty routine:

- ○ Will you provide hair and makeup services to your entire wedding party?

- ○ Where will the team work? Will you travel to a salon or have the team come to you?

- ○ How formal do you want to go? Do you want just a sleek blow-out? Do you have a vision of an elaborate updo or long waves enhanced by extensions?

- ○ For makeup, are you thinking of a glamorous runway look or just a step up from your own natural look?

- ○ Is it important to you that your attendants have a uniform look?

- ○ Will the team work with your mother and the mother of the groom?

As always, ask for references before you sign a contract. Hair stylists and makeup artists should have lots of photos to show their work. And, most importantly, schedule a trial run with each stylist well in advance of the big day.

BRIDAL BEAUTY WORKSHEET

HAIRSTYLIST

NAME:

PHONE: EMAIL:

HAIR CONSULTATIONS/TRIALS

DATE: TIME: DATE: TIME:

HAIR WEDDING DAY APPOINTMENT

LOCATION:

TIME: NUMBER OF HOURS:

SERVICES INCLUDED

COST

TOTAL COST OF SERVICES: $

OVERTIME COST: $

TRAVEL FEE: $

NOTES

MAKEUP ARTIST

NAME:

PHONE: EMAIL:

MAKEUP CONSULTATIONS/TRIALS

DATE: TIME: DATE: TIME:

MAKEUP WEDDING DAY APPOINTMENT

LOCATION:

TIME: NUMBER OF HOURS:

SERVICES INCLUDED

13

COST

TOTAL COST OF SERVICES: $

OVERTIME COST: $

TRAVEL FEE: $

NOTES

NAIL TECHNICIAN

NAME:

PHONE: EMAIL:

NAIL CONSULTATIONS/TRIALS

DATE: TIME: DATE: TIME:

NAIL WEDDING DAY APPOINTMENT

LOCATION:

TIME: NUMBER OF HOURS:

SERVICES INCLUDED

COST

TOTAL COST OF SERVICES: $

TRAVEL FEE: $

NOTES

13

CHAPTER 14

The Music

Carefully selected music can provide atmosphere and enhance the mood and meaning of your ceremony. You may already have an auditory fantasy of the music that will be playing as you walk down the aisle, as you take your vows, and as you leave the ceremony. It's your wedding day; choose the music that will make it feel right for both of you. However, if you are planning on having a church ceremony, bear in mind that some places of worship have restrictions on what kind of music is and is not allowed, so be sure to check with your officiant before you set your heart on walking down the aisle to a particular tune.

14

THE PRELUDE

The prelude lasts from the time the guests start arriving until all of them are seated and the mother of the bride (traditionally the last-seated guest before the wedding party comes down the aisle) is ready to make her entrance. The prelude establishes a mood and entertains the guests while they wait. The end of the prelude, right before the processional, is usually a good time for a soloist or choir to break into song. During the final piece of the prelude, the mother of the bride is seated. Some good classical choices for the prelude include:

- Handel's *Water Music*
- Mozart's "Adagio" from *Ave verum corpus*
- Vivaldi's "Largo" from "Winter" (*The Four Seasons*)
- Bach's *Brandenburg Concertos*
- Bach's "Jesu, Joy of Man's Desiring"
- Bach's Eight Short Preludes and Fugues for the Organ
- Mendelssohn's "Adagio" from Organ Sonata No. 2
- Peeters's "Aria" from Sonata for Trumpet and Piano
- Massenet's "Méditation" from the opera *Thaïs*

14

THE PROCESSIONAL

The processional is the music that accompanies the wedding party as they walk down the aisle. When it's time for you to enter, you can walk to the same piece that you've chosen for the attendants or choose something different. Sometimes, the piece is the same but is played at a different tempo or with an audience-captivating pause before it begins. Brides differ widely in their preferences for their processional pieces. Here are some timeless suggestions:

- Wagner's "Bridal Chorus" ("Here comes the bride...") from the opera *Lohengrin*

- Mendelssohn's "Wedding March" from *A Midsummer Night's Dream* suite

- Bach's "Sheep may safely graze"

- Stanley's "Trumpet Voluntary"

- Pachelbel's Canon in D

- Handel's "Hornpipe" from *Water Music* suite

- Charpentier's "Prelude" from Te Deum

CEREMONY MUSIC

The perfect choice of music played during the actual wedding ceremony can enhance the mood and highlight the significance of the occasion. If you're getting married in a church, chances are your musical choices will be limited to Christian religious songs. Some songs to consider are the following:

- Schubert's "Ave Maria"

- Artman's "Wedding Prayer"

- Malotte's "The Lord's Prayer"

- Wetherill's "A Marriage Prayer"

- Traditional, "The Irish Wedding Song"

- Franck's "Panis Angelicus"

- Callahan's "Wherever You Go"

- Dvořák's "God Is My Shepherd"

- Peeters's "Wedding Song: Whither Thou Goest, There Will I Go Also"

14

THE RECESSIONAL

The exit song should be joyous and upbeat, reflecting your happiness at being joined together as you walk down the aisle and outside. An upbeat song will also help move your guests along outside more quickly than a sedate piece.

Many of the processional pieces previously listed can be used at either the beginning or the end of the ceremony. Some other classic suggestions include the following:

- ⚪ Widor's "Toccata" from Symphony for Organ No. 5
- ⚪ Purcell's "Trumpet Tune"
- ⚪ Willan's "Finale Jubilante" from Five Pieces
- ⚪ Handel's "Sinfonia (The Arrival of the Queen of Sheba)" from the oratorio Solomon
- ⚪ Vierne's "Finale" from Organ Symphony No. 1
- ⚪ Wesley's "Choral Song and Fugue"

If you're marrying in a place of worship, the officiant will most likely be able to suggest musicians they've worked with in the past. Be sure to take the time to listen to the musicians before agreeing to hire them. You may prefer to bring in outside performers. A nonreligious ceremony will also need music. Check with the venue manager or wedding planner for suggestions. Or check out the music department of your local college or university to find talented musicians and singers.

14

CEREMONY MUSIC WORKSHEET

MUSICIAN

NAME:	INSTRUMENT:
PHONE:	EMAIL:
FEE: $	

SOLOIST

NAME:	INSTRUMENT:
PHONE:	EMAIL:
FEE: $	

OTHER MUSICIAN(S), IF APPLICABLE

NAME:	INSTRUMENT:
PHONE:	EMAIL:
FEE: $	
NAME:	INSTRUMENT:
PHONE:	EMAIL:
FEE: $	

COST

TOTAL AMOUNT DUE:	$	
AMOUNT OF DEPOSIT:	$	DATE:
BALANCE DUE:	$	DATE:

MUSIC TO BE PLAYED DURING CEREMONY

PART OF CEREMONY	MUSICAL SELECTION	PERFORMED BY
PRELUDE:		
PROCESSIONAL:		
DURING THE CEREMONY: (list specific part here)		
RECESSIONAL:		
OTHER:		

14

THE RECEPTION

The big decision about music for the reception is whether to hire a band or a DJ. When it comes to price, a DJ is usually the less expensive option, but there are other factors that may influence your choice. Whichever you choose, you will want to finalize arrangements approximately six months in advance of your wedding date.

LIVE BANDS

If you're lucky enough to already know of live musicians who can work within your budget, book them quickly—before another bride hires your band for her wedding. If you're not so lucky, plan to make many treks to bars, lounges, and function halls—any place where you might find some decent live music. In addition to the band's sound, look for a variety of musical styles and tempos in their repertoire. Do they play seven slow songs, one fast number, then two more slow ones, or do they know how to vary the pace? Do they appear to be enjoying themselves, or do they look like they'd rather be somewhere else?

Once you find a band you like, make arrangements with the leader to sit down and talk about exactly what you want concerning your wedding. Have a list of songs ready that they absolutely must play at your reception. If they don't know the songs already, will they attempt to learn them in time? Ask about their sound system and equipment needs. If your reception site is too small or doesn't have the proper electrical outlets and fuse power, it's better to know before you hire the band.

Before you sign a contract with the band, make sure the following commitments are stipulated in writing:

- The cost of hiring the band and everything included in that price
- The band's attire
- Arrival and set-up time
- The length of playing time

14

DJS

DJs can obviously provide more variety than bands and give you the original version of songs, and they don't cause as many logistical headaches. Most people see DJs as slightly less formal than bands, but they're also considerably less expensive, which adds a great deal to their appeal.

If possible, try to see and hear a DJ in action. Look for the same things you would in a band: balance, variety, a good mix of fast and slow songs, an appealing personality, and first-rate equipment. Could this person perform the duties of a master of ceremonies? Do they talk way too much or far too little?

Your disc jockey should be able to accommodate the majority of your guests' requests. Provide a list of what you want to be played at the reception, and if there are some songs you absolutely do not want to be played, give them a (short) list of those too. However, be prepared to compromise and trust the DJ's musical judgment. Their main interest is playing music that will jump-start your party and keep it going. Some other questions to ask your DJ include the following:

- How many weddings have they provided music for? What size wedding do they typically work?
- Can they provide a wireless microphone for any toasts or speeches?
- Will they provide appropriate music for the cocktail hour?
- Is the gratuity included in the price?

The DJ's exact cost, including possible extras, the time of arrival and departure, the place, and their proper attire should all be spelled out in the contract. It is also possible that your DJ will have to sign another agreement with your reception site; these agreements typically involve what time the DJ is permitted to enter the facility and set up, noise control, speaker wattage, and what kinds of equipment they are permitted to use.

RECEPTION MUSIC WORKSHEET

NAME OF BAND/DJ:

ADDRESS:

PHONE: EMAIL:

CONTACT: NUMBER OF PERFORMERS:

DESCRIPTION OF ACT

DEMO AVAILABLE?   ☐ Yes   ☐ No

VIEW LIVE PERFORMANCE?   ☐ Yes   ☐ No

DATE: TIME:

LOCATION:

NOTES

APPOINTMENTS

DATE: TIME:

DATE: TIME:

DATE: TIME:

WEDDING DAY INFORMATION

DATE OF HIRED SERVICES: TIME:

NUMBER OF HOURS: COCKTAIL HOUR: ☐ Yes   ☐ No

OVERTIME COSTS: $

INCLUDED SERVICES

14

RECEPTION MUSIC WORKSHEET (CONTINUED)

EQUIPMENT

PROVIDED:	RENTED:

EQUIPMENT COSTS: $

COST

TOTAL AMOUNT DUE: $

AMOUNT OF DEPOSIT: $ DATE:

BALANCE DUE: $ DATE:

TERMS OF CANCELLATION

NOTES

THE SONGS

No matter what kind of musical talent you decide on in the end, you'll need to have an idea of the music you want played during the reception. If you're following tradition and including the first dance with your groom, and then a dance with your dad and the groom's dance with his mother, you'll have to tell your bandleader or DJ which songs you want to hear at those moments.

Your choices for reception music are limited only by your imagination (and possibly by your band's repertoire). Whatever type(s) of music you choose, remember that this entertainment is a little gift to your guests to add to their enjoyment of your wedding. Your best bet is to go with an all-inclusive song list that covers a broad spectrum of musical tastes—slow, dance tunes, rock, and soul.

14

RECEPTION MUSIC LIST

SPECIAL DANCES

FIRST DANCE

FATHER/BRIDE DANCE

MOTHER/GROOM DANCE

OTHER

SONG TO GET EVERYONE OUT ON THE DANCE FLOOR

FAVORITE SONGS

14

SONGS TO SKIP

CHAPTER 15

The Flowers

If you've been knocked out by the floral design at a recent wedding or other special event, ask the host for the florist's contact information. You can also get florist referrals from your reception site coordinator, check out online review hubs, or visit florists' booths at wedding exhibitions.

15

HOW TO GET WHAT YOU WANT

Here are some questions you may want to ask a potential florist to ensure they understand your vision and can meet your expectations:

○ **Availability.** Are they available on the wedding date? How many weddings do they typically handle in a weekend?

○ **Experience.** How long have they been in the floral design business? Have they worked on weddings similar to the style and size of yours?

○ **Portfolio and references.** Can you see photos of previous wedding designs? Can they provide references from past clients?

○ **Budget.** What is their pricing structure? Can you work within your budget?

○ **Customization.** Is the florist open to customizing arrangements based on your preferences? Can they suggest flower options that fit your budget and vision?

○ **Venue familiarity.** Have they worked at your wedding venue before? If not, are they willing to visit the venue ahead of time to plan the arrangements?

○ **Floral design style.** What is their signature style? Can they accommodate specific themes or styles you have in mind?

○ **Logistics.** How will the flowers be transported to the venue? How far in advance do they typically set up the floral arrangements?

○ **Delivery and setup.** Will they personally handle the delivery and setup of the arrangements? What is their policy if there are any issues with the flowers on the day of the wedding?

○ **Cancellations.** What is their policy for cancellations or changes in the floral arrangements? How far in advance do you need to finalize the details?

15

Contract and payments. Can you see a sample contract? What is their payment schedule?

Contingency plans. What happens if there are unexpected issues, such as flower unavailability? Do they have a backup plan for emergencies?

Seasonal availability. Can they recommend flowers that are in season during your wedding? How do seasonal changes affect the availability and cost of flowers?

Additional services. Do they provide other services, such as preserving the bouquet or providing additional decor elements?

Once you pick a florist, you'll need a written contract stipulating costs, times, dates, places, and services. Make sure the florist is scheduled to arrive before the photographer on your wedding day, so the flowers will be in the photos.

15

FLORIST WORKSHEET

FLORIST (OPTION 1)

NAME:

ADDRESS:

PHONE: EMAIL:

CONTACT:

APPOINTMENTS

DATE: TIME:

DATE: TIME:

DATE: TIME:

INCLUDED SERVICES

COST

TRAVEL FEE: $

ADDITIONAL FEE: $

TOTAL AMOUNT DUE: $

AMOUNT OF DEPOSIT: $ DATE:

BALANCE DUE: $ DATE:

TERMS OF CANCELLATION

15

NOTES

FLORIST (OPTION 2)

NAME:

ADDRESS:

PHONE: EMAIL:

CONTACT:

APPOINTMENTS

DATE: TIME:

DATE: TIME:

DATE: TIME:

INCLUDED SERVICES

COST

TRAVEL FEE: $

ADDITIONAL FEE: $

TOTAL AMOUNT DUE: $

AMOUNT OF DEPOSIT: $ DATE:

BALANCE DUE: $ DATE:

TERMS OF CANCELLATION

15

NOTES

WHAT DO YOU NEED?

The specific arrangements you need for your wedding depend on your preferences, your budget, and the size and formality of your wedding. Here are the most common floral arrangements for weddings:

○ **Bridal bouquet.** The bride's bouquet is a focal point and should complement the bride's dress and overall theme. It's usually larger or more elaborate than bridesmaid bouquets.

○ **Bridesmaid bouquets.** Smaller than the bride's bouquet but coordinated with the overall color scheme and style.

○ **Groom's boutonniere.** A small floral arrangement worn on the groom's lapel, matching the bridal bouquet or the overall theme.

○ **Corsages.** Worn by mothers and grandmothers of the bride and groom, as well as other special female guests.

○ **Groomsmen boutonnieres.** Similar to the groom's boutonniere but typically smaller and simpler.

○ **Ceremony decor.** Floral arrangements for the ceremony venue, such as altar or arch decorations, aisle markers, or pew arrangements.

○ **Reception centerpieces.** Table centerpieces for guest tables at the reception. These can vary in size and style, from elaborate floral arrangements to simple and elegant designs.

○ **Head table decor.** Special floral arrangements for the head table where the bride, groom, and bridal party sit. You may want to simply place your bouquet in a vase if its size allows for this.

○ **Cake flowers.** Small floral arrangements or edible flowers used to decorate the wedding cake and/or dessert table.

15

○ **Entrance and foyer decor.** Floral arrangements placed at the entrance of the ceremony and reception venues as well as in foyer areas.

○ **Buffet or bar decor.** Floral arrangements placed near food stations or the bar for added decoration.

○ **Throwaway bouquet.** A smaller bouquet similar to the bride's bouquet, meant to be tossed to single women during the bouquet toss tradition.

○ **Aisle decor.** Floral arrangements or petals scattered along the aisle to create a beautiful pathway for the bride. If you are having a flower girl, ask about a basket of petals.

○ **Hanging installations.** Hanging floral arrangements or installations can add a unique and visually striking element to both the ceremony and reception spaces.

○ **Guest book table decor.** A small arrangement on the table where guests sign in or leave messages.

15

WEDDING PARTY FLOWERS WORKSHEET

ITEM/PERSON	DESCRIPTION	NUMBER	COST
BRIDE AND BRIDE'S ATTENDANTS			
BOUQUET			
☐ Bride			$
☐ Maid/Matron of Honor			$
☐ Bridesmaids			$
☐ Flower Girl			$
THROW AWAY BOUQUET			
☐ Bride			$
HEADPIECE			
☐ Bride			$
☐ Maid/Matron of Honor			$
☐ Bridesmaids			$
☐ Flower Girl			$
EXTRA FLOWERS AND/OR BASKET			
☐ Flower Girl			$
GROOM AND GROOM'S ATTENDANTS			
BOUTONNIERE			
☐ Groom			$
☐ Best Man			$
☐ Ushers			$
☐ Ring Bearer			$
RING PILLOW/OTHER			
☐ Ring Bearer			$

15

ITEM/PERSON	DESCRIPTION	NUMBER	COST
FAMILY			
CORSAGE			
☐ Mother of the Bride			$
☐ Mother of the Groom			$
☐ Other			$
BOUTONNIERE			
☐ Father of the Bride			$
☐ Father of the Groom			$
☐ Other			$
OTHER			
			$
			$
			$
			$
			$
Total:			$

15

CEREMONY FLOWERS AND DECORATIONS WORKSHEET

ITEM	DESCRIPTION	NUMBER	COST
AISLE RUNNER			$
ALTAR FLOWERS			$
GARLAND			$
POTTED FLOWERS			$
POTTED PLANTS			$
PEWS/CHAIR FLOWERS			$
PEWS/CHAIR BOWS			$
CANDELABRA			$
CANDLEHOLDERS			$
CANDLES			$
UNITY CANDLE			$
WEDDING ARCH			$
COLUMNS			$
TRELLIS			$
WREATHS			$
OTHER			$
			$
			$
			$
			$
			$
			$
			$
Total:			$

RECEPTION FLOWERS AND DECORATIONS WORKSHEET

ITEM/TABLE	DESCRIPTION	NUMBER	COST
MAIN DECOR			
CENTERPIECES			
☐ Head Table			$
☐ Guest Tables			$
GARLAND			
☐ Head Table			$
☐ Guest Tables			$
☐ Buffet Table			$
☐ Cake Table			$
CANDLES			
☐ Head Table			$
☐ Guest Tables			$
FLOWERS			
☐ Buffet Table			$
☐ Cake Table			$
☐ Guest Book Table			$
DECORATIONS			
☐ Buffet Table			$
☐ Cake Table			$
☐ Guest Book Table			$

15

RECEPTION FLOWERS AND DECORATIONS WORKSHEET
(CONTINUED)

ITEM/TABLE	DESCRIPTION	NUMBER	COST
OTHER			
CANDELABRA			$
CANDLEHOLDERS			$
CANDLES			$
ARCHWAY			$
COLUMNS			$
TRELLIS			$
WREATHS			$
GARLANDS			$
POTTED FLOWERS			$
POTTED PLANTS			$
HANGING PLANTS			$
OTHER			$
			$
			$
			$
			$
			$
Total:			**$**

15

CHAPTER 16

The Photographer and Videographer

A picture is worth a thousand words. At no time in your life will this statement seem truer or more appropriate than on your wedding day. You'll be feeling things you can't even recognize, never mind describe—and thanks to the art of photography, you won't have to. A good set of wedding photos and a professionally shot video will preserve all the emotions, excitement, and memories for you and your friends and family.

16

FINDING A PHOTOGRAPHER

It's common for the best photographers to be booked a year or more in advance, so start your search early. Begin with the word-of-mouth approach. Ask your friends, family, coworkers, or anyone else you know who has recently coordinated a wedding. When you have the names of a few good photographers, look at their website galleries to see what kind of work they do.

It also goes without saying that you're looking for someone who knows what they are doing. So how can you grade the photographer's abilities if you don't even know how to work a camera that isn't part of a cell phone? For starters, look for crispness and composition. Did the photographer make good use of lighting? Were a variety of backgrounds and settings used? Do they seem to be well versed in the style you're looking for? This should give you an idea of what to look for, but if you have a friend or family member who knows photography, bring them along with you on the interview with the photographer.

Don't be afraid to ask a lot of questions when you interview a photographer. Find out before you sign a contract what you're getting into. Ask:

- How long has the photographer been in business?
- Do they specialize in weddings?
- Will they have a second shooter to capture special moments from different angles?
- What kinds of packages are offered? What's included in each package?
- How many pictures do they typically take at a wedding of your size?
- Is there an hourly rate or a flat fee?
- Will you be able to purchase additional photos in the future?
- What are the costs for additional photos or online hosting?

Look at some of the photographer's recent work. Ask for references and make sure you call the references to ask about their experience.

16

PHOTOGRAPHER WORKSHEET

PHOTOGRAPHER/STUDIO

NAME:

ADDRESS:

PHONE: EMAIL:

CONTACT:

APPOINTMENTS

DATE: TIME:

DATE: TIME:

DATE: TIME:

PACKAGE INFORMATION

NAME OF PACKAGE:

NUMBER OF PHOTOS:

ENGAGEMENT SESSION INCLUDED?   ☐ Yes   ☐ No

ADDTL. COST, IF ANY: $

WILL ATTEND REHEARSAL?   ☐ Yes   ☐ No

ADDTL. COST, IF ANY: $

TYPE OF WEDDING ALBUM INCLUDED:

DATE OF HIRED SERVICES: TIME:

NUMBER OF HOURS:

OVERTIME COST: $

DATE PHOTOS WILL BE AVAILABLE FOR VIEWING:

INCLUDED SERVICES

16

FEES

TRAVEL:	$	WEBSITE:	$
CUSTOM PAGES:	$	PER FLASH DRIVE:	$
ALBUM INSCRIPTION:	$	OTHER:	$

COST

TOTAL AMOUNT DUE:	$		
AMOUNT OF DEPOSIT:	$	DATE:	
BALANCE DUE:	$	DATE:	

TERMS OF CANCELLATION

NOTES

WORKING WITH THE PHOTOGRAPHER

After you've chosen the photographer, sit down and discuss your wants, needs, and expectations. It's important to establish a good relationship well before the wedding so that everyone feels comfortable when the big, frenzied day arrives. There are, of course, traditional wedding poses and shots, but if you have anything else in mind, let your photographer know. Provide a list of all of the special people you want included in the pictures, especially anyone who isn't in the wedding party.

16

CHOOSE A STYLE

The photojournalistic style is probably the most popular option for wedding pictures. These are the photos that appear to be taken when no one's paying attention, and they can produce some unforgettable images. Emotions are captured in a more natural state. Tight shots blend with wide scenes to truly tell the entire story of the day. Many couples do a hybrid of traditional, posed shots with photojournalistic pictures. If you're interested in this style, however, be sure to ask your photographer if they have done these shots in the past and ask to see samples.

SHOOTING ON LOCATION

Some couples opt to take their formal wedding photos at a location other than the reception site. Sometimes, the spot they select is of great sentimental value; sometimes, it's chosen just because the scenery is gorgeous. If you do plan to take your photo shoot on the road, remember that your guests will have to wait even longer than usual to see you at the reception. Make sure that the reception site will be offering bar service and hors d'oeuvres while guests wait for you to arrive. Another, simpler option is to take the majority of your family and attendant pictures before the ceremony.

PHOTOGRAPHIC EXTRAS

Aside from working with you on the wedding day, you may want the photographer to do an engagement shoot or schedule a formal bridal portrait. If so, you'll need to iron out the details with the photographer at your initial meeting.

16

PHOTOGRAPH CHECKLIST

NAME OF BRIDE AND GROOM:

PHONE:

WEDDING DATE:

CEREMONY LOCATION:

RECEPTION LOCATION:

SPECIAL INSTRUCTIONS

PORTRAITS

- [ ] Bride and groom during the ceremony
- [ ] An official wedding portrait of the bride and groom
- [ ] The entire wedding party
- [ ] Bride, groom, and family members
- [ ] Bride and mother
- [ ] Bride and father
- [ ] Bride and both parents
- [ ] Bride with groom's parents
- [ ] Groom and mother

- [ ] Groom and father
- [ ] Groom and both parents
- [ ] Groom with bride's parents
- [ ] Combination photos of the attendants
- [ ] Bride and groom with special guests, such as grandparents or godparents
- [ ] Other:

16

PHOTOS FROM THE CEREMONY

- [ ] Each member of the wedding party walking down the aisle
- [ ] Mother of the bride as she is ushered down the aisle
- [ ] Groom's parents
- [ ] Bride and father walking down the aisle
- [ ] Bride and father at the altar
- [ ] Wedding party at the altar
- [ ] Ring exchange
- [ ] The vows
- [ ] Candle lighting or special ceremony features
- [ ] Readings
- [ ] The kiss
- [ ] The walk from the altar
- [ ] Other:

CANDIDS

- [ ] Getting ready for the ceremony
- [ ] The bridesmaids and bride before the wedding
- [ ] Bride and father leaving
- [ ] Bride and father arriving at the ceremony
- [ ] Getting out of the limousine/car
- [ ] First look
- [ ] Bride and groom getting in the car
- [ ] Toasting one another in the car
- [ ] Reception arrival
- [ ] Toasts
- [ ] First dance
- [ ] Cutting the cake
- [ ] Guests dancing
- [ ] Informal groupings (siblings, college friends, coworkers, cousins, etc.)
- [ ] Bouquet toss
- [ ] Garter toss
- [ ] Going-away dance
- [ ] Leaving for the honeymoon
- [ ] Other:

16

FINDING A VIDEOGRAPHER

The bride and groom are, ironically, the two people who usually remember the least about their wedding. They're in a fog of emotion and excitement, in which hundreds of sensory impressions go by in a blur. Still photographs will show you a few staged poses, but video will show how things were. You can have a record of the guests as they sing, dance, eat, kiss, cry, and laugh. When you finally sit down to watch your wedding video, it will certainly bring back memories, but it will also show you many things you were not able to notice during the wedding.

Plan on interviewing a few videographers so you can find exactly what you're looking for. Confirm that your videographer has up-to-date, quality equipment. Ask about editing and dubbing, microphones, and lights. Find out how many cameras they will use and how many people will be working on the job.

Ask to view samples. You're looking for smooth editing, clear sound, and an overall professional look and feel to the video. Ask for the names of former clients and call to them find out if they were satisfied with the wedding day filming and the final product. Remember that it's in your best interest to ask as many questions as you need. Here are some things to ask:

- How long has the videographer been in business?
- Do they specialize in weddings?
- What kinds of packages are offered? What's included in each package?
- Is there an hourly rate or a flat fee?
- Will the final video include music, subtitles, or any special effects?
- How will the video be transferred to you?
- What are the costs for additional photos, flash drives, online hosting, or DVDs?

Once you've found someone and verified references, get a written contract stipulating costs, services, operators, and, of course, the date, time, and place.

16

VIDEOGRAPHER WORKSHEET

VIDEOGRAPHER/STUDIO:

ADDRESS:

PHONE: EMAIL:

CONTACT:

APPOINTMENTS

DATE: TIME:

DATE: TIME:

DATE: TIME:

PACKAGE INFORMATION

NAME OF PACKAGE:

LENGTH OF VIDEO:

WILL ATTEND REHEARSAL?   ☐ Yes   ☐ No

ADDTL. COST, IF ANY: $

DATE OF HIRED SERVICES: TIME:

NUMBER OF CAMERAS:

NUMBER OF HOURS:

OVERTIME COST: $

DATE VIDEO WILL BE READY

VIDEO FOOTAGE INCLUDES

Sound: ☐ Yes   ☐ No   NOTES:

Music: ☐ Yes   ☐ No

Unedited Version of Events: ☐ Yes   ☐ No

NOTES:

Edited Version of Events: ☐ Yes   ☐ No

NOTES:

Other:

NOTES:

16

DVD INCLUDES

☐ Pre-wedding preparations

☐ Individual interviews with bride and groom before ceremony

☐ Ceremony

☐ Reception

☐ Photo montage

☐ Other:

NOTES:

NUMBER OF INCLUDED COPIES:

ADDITIONAL COPIES: $

COST

TRAVEL FEE: $

ADDITIONAL FEES: $

TOTAL AMOUNT DUE: $

AMOUNT OF DEPOSIT: $ DATE:

BALANCE DUE: $ DATE:

SALES TAX INCLUDED?   ☐ Yes   ☐ No

TERMS OF CANCELLATION

NOTES

16

CHAPTER 17

The Transportation

Most brides picture themselves arriving in style at the door of the wedding site. If you're going to need a ride to the ceremony, you'll have to start looking for transportation as soon as possible. And if you're thinking about ditching the limo in favor of a plane ride to a destination wedding, you'll need to think about how you're going to get your dress there on time (not to mention your guests).

17

LIMOUSINES

Limousines are the most common mode of wedding transportation. They provide a comfortable, roomy ride, along with a professional driver. Here are some things to consider when planning your wedding transportation:

○ How many cars will you need? If you're on a budget and don't mind having the wedding party arrive at different times, you can get by with just one limo (and a tight schedule). If you can afford more cars, you can transport everyone, including parents and attendants, at the same time.

○ How soon should reservations be made? Generally speaking, it's never too early to look into your transportation options. It's not uncommon for limos to be booked a year in advance; many companies will even take reservations up to a year and a half before an event.

○ Make sure you verify a service's license and insurance coverage. Get references. Verify that the drivers show up on time and are courteous and professional.

○ Inspect the cars. Does the fleet look modern and up-to-date, or do the cars look like they might be on their last legs? The vehicles should be clean and undamaged. The interiors should be spotless and odor-free. And there should be enough room for everyone you're planning on transporting.

○ How are charges calculated? Limousine services typically charge by the hour. Most companies have package deals with a specific number of hours included in the price. Make sure the package time covers the amount of time you need.

○ What else is included in a package? Do they provide champagne, ice, and glasses? A red carpet? Some limo companies can add extras like balloons or flowers.

17

Once you decide on a service, get all the details finalized in a written contract. It should specify the type of car, additional options and services you will need, the expected length of service, the date, and the time. If you've chosen a specific limo, make sure it's specified in the contract. Ask about contingencies. If you're choosing the company's top-of-the-line car and something happens to it, what then? Get this in writing also.

17

TRANSPORTATION WORKSHEET

NAME OF COMPANY:

ADDRESS:

PHONE: EMAIL:

CONTACT:

PACKAGE INFORMATION

NUMBER OF VEHICLES RENTED:

DESCRIPTION:

HOURS OF RENTAL: MINIMUM NUMBER OF HOURS:

COST PER HOUR: $

OVERTIME COST: $

NAME OF DRIVER(S):

INCLUDED SERVICES

COST

TOTAL AMOUNT DUE: $

AMOUNT OF DEPOSIT: $ DATE:

BALANCE DUE: $ DATE:

TERMS OF CANCELLATION

17

NOTES

DRIVER'S CHECKLIST WORKSHEET

VEHICLE: DRIVER:

DATE:

NAME OF BRIDE AND GROOM:

LOCATION #1

PLACE OF PICK UP: ARRIVAL TIME:

NAMES OF PASSENGER(S):

ADDRESS:

PHONE:

SPECIAL INSTRUCTIONS

LOCATION #2

PLACE OF PICK UP: ARRIVAL TIME:

NAMES OF PASSENGER(S):

ADDRESS:

PHONE:

SPECIAL INSTRUCTIONS

LOCATION #3

PLACE OF PICK UP: ARRIVAL TIME:

NAMES OF PASSENGER(S):

ADDRESS:

PHONE:

SPECIAL INSTRUCTIONS

17

DRIVER'S CHECKLIST WORKSHEET (CONTINUED)

LOCATION #4

PLACE OF PICK UP: _____ ARRIVAL TIME: _____

NAMES OF PASSENGER(S): _____

_____

ADDRESS: _____

PHONE: _____

SPECIAL INSTRUCTIONS

_____

_____

LOCATION #5

PLACE OF PICK UP: _____ ARRIVAL TIME: _____

NAMES OF PASSENGER(S): _____

_____

ADDRESS: _____

PHONE: _____

SPECIAL INSTRUCTIONS

_____

_____

17

OTHER OPTIONS

If you don't like the idea of limos and are looking for something different, consider one of these options:

○ **Horse and Carriage.** No matter the season, there's no sight more beautiful than a bride riding to her wedding in a horse-drawn carriage. If you're planning a winter wedding, obviously you will, at the very least, have to invest in a warm wrap.

○ **Shuttles and Trolleys.** A shuttle provides plenty of seating for your entire wedding party at once. This option encourages a fun, casual atmosphere onboard. Trolleys offer the same kind of space as a shuttle bus but in a nicer package. Many trolley rides are open-air affairs, but in colder climates, most provide some kind of protection from the winter elements.

○ **Sleek Rides.** Are you the white Rolls-Royce type? Perhaps a silver Bentley would suit you best. If you've got some extra cash on hand, go all out: Snag an Excalibur. It will make for a truly unforgettable shot in your wedding video. Many limousine companies also have a few classic cars on their lots. You don't have to squeeze your attendants into this car with you—you can hire a limo or SUV just for them.

○ **Free Ride.** If you're unable to rent wedding transportation, look around for family members or friends who have nice big cars they'd be willing to lend you. The only requirement here is that the cars have to be clean. You should pay for the pre-wedding car wash and detailing. And be sure to remember your generous friends with a little gift and a full tank of gas.

17

TRANSPORTING THE ENTIRE WEDDING

If you're planning a wedding on a Caribbean island or somewhere overseas, you're going to be faced with much larger transportation issues. Getting yourself there is the easy part—but what about your dress? If you're inviting guests, are you expected to pay for their transportation too?

The guest list for a destination wedding tends to be small, including only the people you're closest to. The ceremony is the focus of the trip. And when the wedding is over, you don't need to hop on a flight to start your honeymoon. Obviously, a lot of planning goes into a wedding that you're taking on the road. Find yourself a good travel agent or wedding planner who is knowledgeable about destination weddings. They can help not only with travel plans but also with any local requirements for weddings at your destination.

PACKING THE DRESS

When transporting your wedding dress, you can't be careful enough. If you can arrange to have the dress packed and shipped, do it. Courier companies are much better equipped than the average airline to handle fragile items and deliver them in one piece in a timely manner. If you're planning a wedding at a resort that specializes in destination weddings, there will probably be an on-site coordinator who can work with you and will know exactly how to steam those inevitable wrinkles out of the dress on your wedding day.

THE GUESTS

Are you expected to pay for your guests' transportation or lodging? If you're including attendants in the ceremony, their hotel bill is your responsibility, according to traditional wedding etiquette. If you can afford their airfare, that's a nice touch. Everyone else is on their own cost-wise, though it would be a nice gesture to take everyone who has traveled out for dinner one evening.

DESTINATION WEDDING: TRAVEL WORKSHEET

GUESTS

TRAVEL INFORMATION

DATES OF TRAVEL

ARRIVING AT DESTINATION:

DEPARTING FROM DESTINATION:

FLIGHT INFORMATION

AIRLINE: PHONE:

WEBSITE:

DATE AND TIME OF RESERVATIONS:

SEAT NUMBERS:

CONFIRMATION NUMBER:

COST: $

CAR RENTAL INFORMATION

COMPANY: PHONE:

WEBSITE:

DATE AND TIME OF RESERVATIONS:

MAKE AND MODEL:

CONFIRMATION NUMBER:

COST: $

17

RESORT/CRUISE LINE CONTACT

NAME: _____ PHONE: _____

EMAIL: _____

WEBSITE: _____

DATE AND TIME OF RESERVATIONS: _____

NUMBER OF ROOMS RESERVED: _____

CONFIRMATION NUMBER: _____

COST: $ _____

WEDDING DAY INFORMATION

CEREMONY SITE

CEREMONY SITE NAME: _____

WEBSITE: _____

DATE AND TIME OF RESERVATIONS: _____

OFFICIANT: _____

OFFICIANT'S PHONE: _____

OFFICIANT'S EMAIL: _____

COST: $ _____

RECEPTION SITE

RECEPTION SITE NAME: _____

WEBSITE: _____

DATE AND TIME OF RESERVATIONS: _____

CONTACT PERSON: _____

CONTACT PERSON'S PHONE: _____

CONTACT PERSON'S EMAIL: _____

COST: $ _____

FLOWERS/DECORATIONS

TYPE OF FLOWERS: _____

COST: _____

DATE AND TIME OF RESERVATIONS: _____

FLORIST'S PHONE: _____

FLORIST'S EMAIL: _____

COST: $ _____

17

DESTINATION WEDDING: TRAVEL WORKSHEET (CONTINUED)

MUSIC

MUSICIANS/DJ:

COST:

MUSICIANS/DJ'S EMAIL:

MUSICIANS/DJ'S PHONE:

DATE AND TIME OF RESERVATIONS:

COST: $

NOTES

17

CHAPTER 18

The Marriage License

(and Other Legal Documents)

Legal details may not sound exciting, but certain issues, such as deciding on your married name and procuring the marriage license, need to be addressed. There's also a bigger concern that may warrant some attention in your relationship: the prenuptial agreement. These aren't necessarily fun tasks, but taking care of them gets you one step closer to the altar.

18

CHANGING YOUR NAME

If you've decided to take on a new name, you'll have some paperwork to deal with. Signing your name on the marriage license is proof of your new name. Now you just have to inform the appropriate people. Wait until you've received a copy of your marriage license before you attempt to change your name on accounts or documents. Your first concerns should be these:

○ Driver's license

○ Social Security card

○ Credit cards

○ Bank accounts and loans

○ Car registration

○ Passport

○ Insurance

BRIDE'S NAME/ADDRESS CHANGE WORKSHEET				
		NOTIFIED OF		
INFORMATION TO BE CHANGED	NAME OF INSTITUTION	Name Change?	Change of Address?	Change in Marital Status?
401(K) ACCOUNTS		☐	☐	☐
CAR INSURANCE		☐	☐	☐
BANK ACCOUNTS		☐	☐	☐
BILLING ACCTS		☐	☐	☐
CAR REGISTRATION		☐	☐	☐
MEMBERSHIPS		☐	☐	☐
CREDIT CARDS		☐	☐	☐
DENTIST		☐	☐	☐
DOCTORS		☐	☐	☐
DRIVER'S LICENSE		☐	☐	☐

18

INFORMATION TO BE CHANGED	NAME OF INSTITUTION	NOTIFIED OF		
		Name Change?	Change of Address?	Change in Marital Status?
EMPLOYMENT		☐	☐	☐
RENTER INSURANCE		☐	☐	☐
HOME INSURANCE		☐	☐	☐
IRA ACCOUNTS		☐	☐	☐
LEASES		☐	☐	☐
LIFE INSURANCE		☐	☐	☐
LOANS		☐	☐	☐
MED. INSURANCE		☐	☐	☐
ALT. INSURANCE		☐	☐	☐
PASSPORT		☐	☐	☐
POST OFFICE		☐	☐	☐
PROPERTY TITLES		☐	☐	☐
SOCIAL SECURITY		☐	☐	☐
STOCKS/BONDS		☐	☐	☐
SUBSCRIPTIONS		☐	☐	☐
TELEPHONE		☐	☐	☐
VOTER RECORDS		☐	☐	☐
WILLS/TRUSTS		☐	☐	☐
OTHER		☐	☐	☐

18

GROOM'S NAME/ADDRESS CHANGE WORKSHEET

INFORMATION TO BE CHANGED	NAME OF INSTITUTION	NOTIFIED OF		
		Name Change?	Change of Address?	Change in Marital Status?
401(K) ACCOUNTS		☐	☐	☐
CAR INSURANCE		☐	☐	☐
BANK ACCOUNTS		☐	☐	☐
BILLING ACCTS		☐	☐	☐
CAR REGISTRATION		☐	☐	☐
MEMBERSHIPS		☐	☐	☐
CREDIT CARDS		☐	☐	☐
DENTIST		☐	☐	☐
DOCTORS		☐	☐	☐
DRIVER'S LICENSE		☐	☐	☐
EMPLOYMENT		☐	☐	☐
RENTER INSURANCE		☐	☐	☐
HOME INSURANCE		☐	☐	☐
IRA ACCOUNTS		☐	☐	☐
LEASES		☐	☐	☐
LIFE INSURANCE		☐	☐	☐
LOANS		☐	☐	☐
MED. INSURANCE		☐	☐	☐
ALT. INSURANCE		☐	☐	☐
PASSPORT		☐	☐	☐

18

| | | NOTIFIED OF | | |
INFORMATION TO BE CHANGED	NAME OF INSTITUTION	Name Change?	Change of Address?	Change in Marital Status?
POST OFFICE		☐	☐	☐
PROPERTY TITLES		☐	☐	☐
SOCIAL SECURITY		☐	☐	☐
STOCKS/BONDS		☐	☐	☐
SUBSCRIPTIONS		☐	☐	☐
TELEPHONE		☐	☐	☐
VOTER RECORDS		☐	☐	☐
WILLS/TRUSTS		☐	☐	☐
OTHER		☐	☐	☐

18

MARRIAGE LICENSE

The criteria for obtaining a marriage license vary not only from state to state but also from county to county within a single state. Before you get your marriage license, find out how long the license will be valid. In some regions, the license is valid for several weeks, while in others, it never expires. Regardless of where you get married, you should be aware of some guidelines for the marriage license. Every state requires the following:

- **Paperwork.** You'll need some sort of valid identification (birth certificate, driver's license, proof of age, proof of citizenship). You must provide proof of divorce or annulment in the case of a second marriage.

- **Fee.** Every state charges a fee. Be aware that many states will accept only cash as payment.

- **Minimum age.** In most areas, you need to be at least eighteen.

- **Waiting period.** Again, this varies by state. Some states require a waiting period of several days between obtaining the license and saying, "I do." In other areas, you can get the license and be married on the same day.

Your best bet is to make a call to your county clerk's office or check their website.

Having a marriage license doesn't mean you are legally married. It means you have the state's permission to get married. To be valid and binding, the license has to be signed by a religious or civil official. The officiant simply signs the license after the completion of the ceremony and sends it back to the proper state office. *Now* you're married!

18

MARRIAGE LICENSE CHECKLIST

PAPERWORK

To file for a marriage license, you will need one or more of the following.
(Check your state and county guidelines for the specific requirements in
your area.)

VALID IDENTIFICATION

☐ Driver's license   ☐ Social Security card

☐ Birth certificate   ☐ Passport

☐ Military ID card   ☐ Other:

DIVORCE/ANNULMENT INFORMATION

☐ Proof of divorce or annulment (if applicable)

FEE

☐ Application fee: $

IMPORTANT LICENSE INFORMATION

DATE FILED FOR MARRIAGE LICENSE ON:

LOCATION WHERE MARRIAGE LICENSE IS STORED FOR SAFEKEEPING:

NOTES

18

PRENUPTIAL AGREEMENTS

Prenuptial agreements aren't just for people with lots of money. They're also used to protect assets such as family businesses or to safeguard the interests of children from a previous marriage. Many parents want to make sure that their children's inheritance is never an issue in the event of divorce or death.

Agreements basically cover the assets, debts, and incomes of each spouse. They might also address any inheritances that either spouse receives during the marriage, tax issues, living arrangements, and will beneficiaries. A prenuptial agreement should include the following elements:

- Full, written disclosure of the assets and liabilities of each party

- Reasonable terms for both parties

- Adequate time for the parties to review the terms with their own lawyers

18

PRENUPTIAL AGREEMENT CHECKLIST

NAME OF LAW FIRM/ATTORNEYS:

ADDRESS:

PHONE: _____ EMAIL: _____

MEETINGS

DATE: _____ TIME: _____

DATE: _____ TIME: _____

ASSETS/LIABILITIES

BRIDE'S ASSETS	BRIDE'S LIABILITIES
GROOM'S ASSETS	GROOM'S LIABILITIES

SPECIFIC ISSUES TO BE ADDRESSED IN AGREEMENT

BRIDE'S CONCERNS	GROOM'S CONCERNS

18

NEWSPAPER WEDDING ANNOUNCEMENT WORKSHEET

PUBLICATION NAME: _____

DATE ANNOUNCEMENT TO APPEAR IN PUBLICATION: _____

NAME(S) OF SENDER: _____

ADDRESS: _____

CONTACT PERSON: _____

PHONE: _____ EMAIL: _____

_____ and _____
(bride's first, middle, and maiden names)   (groom's first, middle, and last names)

were married at _____ in _____ .
                (name of church or synagogue)   (city or town)

The bride, _____ , is the daughter of
            (optional: name change information; for example, "will continue to use her surname")

Mr. and Mrs. _____ of _____ . She graduated
             (bride's parent's name)   (their city, if out of town)

from _____ and is a/an _____ at _____ .
     (optional: name of college or university)   (job title)   (name of employer)

The bridegroom, son of Mr. and Mrs. _____ ,
                                     (groom's parents' names)

of _____ , graduated from _____ and is a/an
   (their city, if out of town)   (optional: name of college or university)

_____ at _____ .
(job title)   (name of employer)

The couple will live in _____ after a trip to _____ .
                        (city or town)   (honeymoon location)

18

CHAPTER 19

The Rehearsal and Rehearsal Dinner

If you're expecting your wedding rehearsal to go something like the final dress rehearsal for a Broadway play, you may be disappointed. You may have the jitters that echo an opening-night panic attack, but your rehearsal will be much less dramatic and nerve-racking than you might think. The rehearsal is mainly a chance for the officiant to meet your wedding party and to acquaint everyone with the basics of the ceremony. And yes, it's very exciting.

THE REHEARSAL

The rehearsal is usually held a night or two before the wedding at the ceremony site. After a brief overview of what's included in the ceremony, the officiant will talk everyone through a quick practice run, starting with the processional, which is at the very beginning of the ceremony. You will decide the order of the attendants walking down the aisle before you.

You'll have a quick run-through of the ceremony, which probably will not include the music but probably will include your readers practicing their parts, or at least where they'll be standing. You and the groom will stand in your places as your officiant goes over the nuptials with you. He will remind you of the appropriate responses to the questions, and if you're going to be reciting your own vows, your officiant will let you know when you'll be expected to speak.

In addition, your honor attendants will be instructed as to their special duties during the ceremony. For instance, your maid of honor will need to take your flowers at a certain point, and your best man will present the rings. And any child-attendant issues can be cleared up at this time, as well. (Is the two-year-old ring bearer going to stay for the entire ceremony, or will he be shuffled out the back door by one of his parents at some point?)

You will practice the recessional, which is your journey out of the ceremony. The bride and groom go first, of course, followed by your attendants and parents, in whichever order you choose.

THE REHEARSAL DINNER

The rehearsal dinner can be as formal or informal as your host wants to make it. It can be held at someone's home, in a restaurant, at a park, on the beach—it can be anywhere. Invitations can be extended by phone, text, or email. There's no need to have special rehearsal dinner invitations printed.

19

Traditionally, the expense of the rehearsal party is borne by the groom's parents. If you and your groom feel uncomfortable asking either set of parents to host this affair (and if no one offers), go ahead and plan it yourselves.

WHO SHOULD ATTEND THE REHEARSAL DINNER?

- Wedding attendants, along with their spouses or significant others
- Parents of the bride and groom
- Siblings of the bride and groom, along with spouses or significant others
- Grandparents of the bride and groom
- The officiant and spouse
- Participants in the ceremony (for example, readers)

You may want to invite other close friends or out-of-town guests, but try to keep this party low-key and relaxing.

SPEECHES

If you follow tradition, toasts will be a part of the evening. If the groom's parents are hosting the rehearsal dinner, the father of the groom offers up a toast to the bride and groom and to the bride's parents. The father of the bride responds with a toast to the hosts and to the almost-newlyweds. The groom then toasts the bride and her family, and the bride responds with a toast to the groom and his family.

Of course, if anyone else wants to make a toast (or someone on that list of toasters would rather not speak publicly), you're not bound to follow the traditional order. And if you prefer to skip the toasts altogether, that's fine too. Remember, there'll be enough formality on the day of the wedding.

19

REHEARSAL CHECKLIST

DATE AND TIME OF REHEARSAL:

ITEMS TO ADDRESS DURING REHEARSAL

- [ ] Bride
- [ ] Officiant
- [ ] Maid of honor
- [ ] Best man
- [ ] Flower girl
- [ ] Readings
- [ ] Special blessings
- [ ] Rings

- [ ] Groom
- [ ] Parents of bride and groom
- [ ] Bridesmaids
- [ ] Groomsmen
- [ ] Ring bearer
- [ ] Readers
- [ ] Gift presenters
- [ ] Marriage license

ADDITIONAL INFORMATION

19

REHEARSAL DINNER WORKSHEET

WEDDING REHEARSAL

LOCATION:

PHONE: CONTACT:

DATE: TIME:

NOTES

DINNER

LOCATION:

PHONE: CONTACT:

DATE: TIME:

NUMBER OF GUESTS:

MENU

BEVERAGES

NOTES

19

REHEARSAL DINNER GUEST LIST WORKSHEET

NAME:	NAME:
ADDRESS:	ADDRESS:
PHONE:	PHONE:
EMAIL:	EMAIL:
☐ RSVP NUMBER IN PARTY:	☐ RSVP NUMBER IN PARTY:
NAME:	NAME:
ADDRESS:	ADDRESS:
PHONE:	PHONE:
EMAIL:	EMAIL:
☐ RSVP NUMBER IN PARTY:	☐ RSVP NUMBER IN PARTY:
NAME:	NAME:
ADDRESS:	ADDRESS:
PHONE:	PHONE:
EMAIL:	EMAIL:
☐ RSVP NUMBER IN PARTY:	☐ RSVP NUMBER IN PARTY:
NAME:	NAME:
ADDRESS:	ADDRESS:
PHONE:	PHONE:
EMAIL:	EMAIL:
☐ RSVP NUMBER IN PARTY:	☐ RSVP NUMBER IN PARTY:
NAME:	NAME:
ADDRESS:	ADDRESS:
PHONE:	PHONE:
EMAIL:	EMAIL:
☐ RSVP NUMBER IN PARTY:	☐ RSVP NUMBER IN PARTY:

19

NAME:	NAME:
ADDRESS:	ADDRESS:
PHONE:	PHONE:
EMAIL:	EMAIL:
☐ RSVP NUMBER IN PARTY:	☐ RSVP NUMBER IN PARTY:

NAME:	NAME:
ADDRESS:	ADDRESS:
PHONE:	PHONE:
EMAIL:	EMAIL:
☐ RSVP NUMBER IN PARTY:	☐ RSVP NUMBER IN PARTY:

NAME:	NAME:
ADDRESS:	ADDRESS:
PHONE:	PHONE:
EMAIL:	EMAIL:
☐ RSVP NUMBER IN PARTY:	☐ RSVP NUMBER IN PARTY:

NAME:	NAME:
ADDRESS:	ADDRESS:
PHONE:	PHONE:
EMAIL:	EMAIL:
☐ RSVP NUMBER IN PARTY:	☐ RSVP NUMBER IN PARTY:

NAME:	NAME:
ADDRESS:	ADDRESS:
PHONE:	PHONE:
EMAIL:	EMAIL:
☐ RSVP NUMBER IN PARTY:	☐ RSVP NUMBER IN PARTY:

19

NAME:

ADDRESS:

PHONE:

EMAIL:

☐ RSVP   NUMBER IN PARTY:

NAME:

ADDRESS:

PHONE:

EMAIL:

☐ RSVP   NUMBER IN PARTY:

NAME:

ADDRESS:

PHONE:

EMAIL:

☐ RSVP   NUMBER IN PARTY:

NAME:

ADDRESS:

PHONE:

EMAIL:

☐ RSVP   NUMBER IN PARTY:

NAME:

ADDRESS:

PHONE:

EMAIL:

☐ RSVP   NUMBER IN PARTY:

NAME:

ADDRESS:

PHONE:

EMAIL:

☐ RSVP   NUMBER IN PARTY:

NAME:

ADDRESS:

PHONE:

EMAIL:

☐ RSVP   NUMBER IN PARTY:

NAME:

ADDRESS:

PHONE:

EMAIL:

☐ RSVP   NUMBER IN PARTY:

NAME:

ADDRESS:

PHONE:

EMAIL:

☐ RSVP   NUMBER IN PARTY:

NAME:

ADDRESS:

PHONE:

EMAIL:

☐ RSVP   NUMBER IN PARTY:

19

NAME:	NAME:
ADDRESS:	ADDRESS:
PHONE:	PHONE:
EMAIL:	EMAIL:
☐ RSVP NUMBER IN PARTY:	☐ RSVP NUMBER IN PARTY:
NAME:	NAME:
ADDRESS:	ADDRESS:
PHONE:	PHONE:
EMAIL:	EMAIL:
☐ RSVP NUMBER IN PARTY:	☐ RSVP NUMBER IN PARTY:
NAME:	NAME:
ADDRESS:	ADDRESS:
PHONE:	PHONE:
EMAIL:	EMAIL:
☐ RSVP NUMBER IN PARTY:	☐ RSVP NUMBER IN PARTY:
NAME:	NAME:
ADDRESS:	ADDRESS:
PHONE:	PHONE:
EMAIL:	EMAIL:
☐ RSVP NUMBER IN PARTY:	☐ RSVP NUMBER IN PARTY:
NAME:	NAME:
ADDRESS:	ADDRESS:
PHONE:	PHONE:
EMAIL:	EMAIL:
☐ RSVP NUMBER IN PARTY:	☐ RSVP NUMBER IN PARTY:

19

CHAPTER 20

The Honeymoon

You'll probably agree that—what with all the frenzied planning, coordinating, organizing, and worrying involved—getting married can feel like a full-time job—and then some. When it's all over with, you'll need more than just an ordinary vacation to recuperate. Your honeymoon is the perfect time to plan the vacation of your dreams.

20

WHAT CAN YOU AFFORD?

Ultimately, your budget will likely have just as much influence as your dreams on your choice of destination. Consult a travel agent or search travel sites to find low-priced airfares, reduced-rate package deals, and other ways to save money. You may be pleasantly surprised. Perhaps you can afford a trip to Hawaii by staying at a less-than-four-star hotel or travel Europe via hostels and off-the-beaten-path Airbnbs.

Some couples who are on strict budgets are happy enough to just get away together, whether that means going camping, arranging for a low-cost visit to a friend's vacation home for the weekend, or taking a quick jaunt to a city an hour away. There's no "right way" to honeymoon, and sometimes, the more creative you have to get, the more romantic the trip can be.

Whether you use a travel agent or make all the honeymoon plans yourself, be sure to keep track of all the details:

- ◯ Transportation reservations
- ◯ Hotel reservations
- ◯ Car rental options or transfers
- ◯ Sites you want to see
- ◯ Activities you want to do

- ◯ Special dinner reservations
- ◯ Contact information for the travel agent, hotel, tour operators, and so on.
- ◯ What to pack

If you need passports for your trip, be sure to apply for them well in advance—at least three or four months ahead of time. Before you leave the country, let your bank and credit card companies know you'll be traveling. You will probably be able to use your credit and debit cards anywhere, but the bank may temporarily suspend your account due to unusual activity. Also consider purchasing travel insurance in case one of you needs medical care while abroad; most American insurance companies won't cover foreign hospital expenses.

20

HONEYMOON BUDGET WORKSHEET				
ITEM	DESCRIPTION	PROJECTED COST	ACTUAL COST	BALANCE DUE
TRANSPORTATION				
AIRFARE		$	$	$
CAR RENTAL		$	$	$
MOPED RENTAL		$	$	$
BIKE RENTAL		$	$	$
TRAIN PASS		$	$	$
TAXI		$	$	$
PARKING FEES		$	$	$
OTHER		$	$	$
ACCOMMODATIONS				
WEDDING NIGHT		$	$	$
DESTINATION		$	$	$
OTHER		$	$	$
FOOD		$	$	$
MEAL PLAN		$	$	$
MEALS		$	$	$
DRINKS		$	$	$
ENTERTAINMENT				
SHOPPING		$	$	$
EXTRA CASH		$	$	$
TIPS		$	$	$
OTHER		$	$	$
Total:				$

TRAVEL ARRANGEMENTS WORKSHEET

TRAVEL AGENCY

NAME OF TRAVEL AGENCY:

ADDRESS:

PHONE: EMAIL:

CONTACT:

NOTES:

CAR RENTAL AGENCY

NAME OF CAR RENTAL AGENCY:

ADDRESS:

PHONE: EMAIL:

CONTACT:

DESCRIPTION OF RESERVED VEHICLE

                                                MAKE/MODEL:

TERMS:

NOTES:

TRANSPORTATION

OPTION #1

DESTINATION:

AIRLINE: FLIGHT/ROUTE:

DEPARTURE DATE: TIME:

ARRIVAL DATE: TIME:

CONFIRMATION NUMBER: DATE:

20

OPTION #2

DESTINATION:

AIRLINE: FLIGHT/ROUTE:

DEPARTURE DATE: TIME:

ARRIVAL DATE: TIME:

CONFIRMATION NUMBER: DATE:

ACCOMMODATIONS

OPTION #1

HOTEL:

ADDRESS:

PHONE: EMAIL:

CONTACT:

CHECK-IN DATE: TIME:

CHECK-OUT DATE: TIME:

TYPE OF ROOM:

DAILY RATE: $

TOTAL COST: $

CONFIRMATION NUMBER: DATE:

OPTION #2

HOTEL:

ADDRESS:

PHONE: EMAIL:

CONTACT:

CHECK-IN DATE: TIME:

CHECK-OUT DATE: TIME:

TYPE OF ROOM:

DAILY RATE: $

TOTAL COST: $

CONFIRMATION NUMBER: DATE:

20

Appendix

WEDDING BUDGET TRACKER

ITEM	COST
WEDDING CONSULTANT	
FEE	$
TIP	$
Wedding Consultant Total:	$
PRE-WEDDING PARTIES	
ENGAGEMENT PARTY	
SITE RENTAL	$
EQUIPMENT RENTAL	$
INVITATIONS	$
FOOD	$
BEVERAGES	$
DECORATIONS	$
FLOWERS	$
PARTY FAVORS	$
Engagement Party Total:	$
BRIDESMAIDS' PARTY/LUNCHEON	
FOOD	$
BEVERAGES	$
DECORATIONS	$
FLOWERS	$
PARTY FAVORS	$
Bridesmaids' Party/Luncheon Party Total:	$
REHEARSAL DINNER	
SITE RENTAL	$
EQUIPMENT RENTAL	$
INVITATIONS	$
FOOD	$
BEVERAGES	$

ITEM	COST
DECORATIONS	$
FLOWERS	$
PARTY FAVORS	$
Rehearsal Dinner Total:	$

CEREMONY	
LOCATION FEE	$
OFFICIANT'S FEE	$
DONATION (OPTIONAL)	$
ORGANIST/ON-SITE MUSICIAN	$
TIP	$
OTHER MUSICIANS	$
TIP	$
PROGRAM	$
CEREMONY TOTAL	$
BUSINESS AND LEGAL MATTERS	$
MARRIAGE LICENSE	$
BLOOD TEST	$
Business and Legal Matters Total:	$

WEDDING JEWELRY	
BRIDE'S WEDDING BAND	$
GROOM'S WEDDING BAND	$
Wedding Jewelry Total:	$

BRIDE'S ATTIRE	
WEDDING GOWN	$
ALTERATIONS	$
UNDERGARMENTS	$
VEIL	$

WEDDING BUDGET TRACKER (CONTINUED)

ITEM	COST
SHOES	$
JEWELRY (EXCLUDING WEDDING RING)	$
MAKEUP ARTIST	$
HAIRSTYLIST	$
NAIL TECHNICIAN	$
Bride's Attire Total:	$

GROOM'S ATTIRE	
TUXEDO	$
SHOES	$
Groom's Attire Total:	$

GIFTS	
BRIDE'S ATTENDANTS	$
GROOM'S ATTENDANTS	$
BRIDE	$
GROOM	$
Gifts Total:	$

RECEPTION	
SITE RENTAL	$
EQUIPMENT RENTAL (CHAIRS, TENT, ETC.)	$
DECORATIONS	$
SERVERS, BARTENDERS	$
WINE SERVICE FOR COCKTAIL HOUR	$
HORS D'OEUVRES	$
ENTRÉES	$
MEALS FOR VENDORS	$
NONALCOHOLIC BEVERAGES	$
WINE	$

WEDDING BUDGET TRACKER (CONTINUED)

ITEM	COST
CHAMPAGNE	$
LIQUOR	$
DESSERT	$
GUEST BOOK	$
PLACE CARDS	$
PRINTED NAPKINS	$
GUEST FAVORS	$
TIP FOR CATERER OR BANQUET MANAGER	$
TIP FOR SERVERS, BARTENDERS	$
Reception Total:	$

PHOTOGRAPHY AND VIDEOGRAPHY

ENGAGEMENT PHOTO SHOOT	$
WEDDING PORTRAIT	$
WEDDING PROOFS	$
PHOTOGRAPHER'S FEE	$
ALBUM	$
MOTHERS' ALBUMS	$
EXTRA PRINTS	$
VIDEOGRAPHER'S FEE	$
Photography and Videography Total:	$

RECEPTION MUSIC

MUSICIANS FOR COCKTAIL HOUR	$
TIP	$
LIVE BAND	$
TIP	$
DISC JOCKEY	$
TIP	$
Reception Music Total:	$

WEDDING BUDGET TRACKER (CONTINUED)

ITEM	COST
FLOWERS AND DECORATIONS	
FLOWERS FOR WEDDING SITE	$
DECORATIONS FOR WEDDING SITE	$
BRIDE'S BOUQUET	$
BRIDESMAIDS' FLOWERS	$
BOUTONNIERES	$
CORSAGES	$
FLOWERS FOR RECEPTION SITE	$
POTTED PLANTS	$
TABLE CENTERPIECES	$
HEAD TABLE	$
CAKE TABLE	$
DECORATIONS FOR RECEPTION	$
Flowers and Decorations Total:	$

ITEM	COST
WEDDING INVITATIONS AND STATIONERY	
INVITATIONS	$
ANNOUNCEMENTS/SAVE THE DATE	$
THANK-YOU NOTES	$
CALLIGRAPHER	$
POSTAGE	$
Wedding Invitations and Stationery Total:	$

ITEM	COST
WEDDING CAKES	
WEDDING CAKE	$
GROOM'S CAKE	$
FLOWERS FOR CAKE	$
Wedding Cakes Total:	$

ITEM	COST
WEDDING TRANSPORTATION	
LIMOUSINES OR RENTED CARS	$
PARKING	$
TIP FOR DRIVERS	$
GUEST TRANSPORTATION	$
Wedding Transportation Total:	$
HONEYMOON	
TRANSPORTATION	$
ACCOMMODATIONS	$
MEALS	$
SPENDING MONEY	$
Honeymoon Total:	$
ADDITIONAL EXPENSES	
	$
	$
	$
	$
	$
	$
	$
	$
	$
	$
	$
Additional Expenses Total:	$
Total of All Expenses:	$

Notes